ROUTLEDGE LIBRARY EDITIONS: POLLUTION, CLIMATE AND CHANGE

Volume 3

A BIBLIOGRAPHY OF THE LITERATURE ON NORTH AMERICAN CLIMATES OF THE PAST 13,000 YEARS

A BIBLIOGRAPHY OF THE LITERATURE ON NORTH AMERICAN CLIMATES OF THE PAST 13,000 YEARS

DONALD K GRAYSON

Taylor & Francis Group

LONDON AND NEW YORK

First published in 1975 by Garland Publishing Inc.

This edition first published in 2020
by Routledge
2 Park Square, Milton Park, Abingdon, Oxon OX14 4RN

and by Routledge
52 Vanderbilt Avenue, New York, NY 10017

Routledge is an imprint of the Taylor & Francis Group, an informa business

© 1975 Donald K. Grayson

All rights reserved. No part of this book may be reprinted or reproduced or utilised in any form or by any electronic, mechanical, or other means, now known or hereafter invented, including photocopying and recording, or in any information storage or retrieval system, without permission in writing from the publishers.

Trademark notice: Product or corporate names may be trademarks or registered trademarks, and are used only for identification and explanation without intent to infringe.

British Library Cataloguing in Publication Data
A catalogue record for this book is available from the British Library

ISBN: 978-0-367-34494-8 (Set)
ISBN: 978-0-429-34741-2 (Set) (ebk)
ISBN: 978-0-367-35921-8 (Volume 3) (hbk)
ISBN: 978-0-367-35925-6 (Volume 3) (pbk)
ISBN: 978-0-429-34262-2 (Volume 3) (ebk)

Publisher's Note
The publisher has gone to great lengths to ensure the quality of this reprint but points out that some imperfections in the original copies may be apparent.

Disclaimer
The publisher has made every effort to trace copyright holders and would welcome correspondence from those they have been unable to trace.

A Bibliography of the Literature on North American Climates of the Past 13,000 Years

Donald K. Grayson

Garland Publishing, Inc., New York & London

1975

Copyright © 1975

by Donald K. Grayson

All Rights Reserved

Library of Congress Cataloging in Publication Data

Grayson, Donald K
  A bibliography of the literature on North American climates of the past 13,000 years.

  (Garland reference library of natural science ; no. 2)
  Includes index.
  1. Paleoclimatology--North America--Bibliography.
I. Title. II. Series.
Z6683.C5G66 1975 [QC982.8]   016.5516'9   75-5131
ISBN 0-8240-9992-3

Printed in the United States of America

Table of Contents

Introduction 6
Acknowledgements.. 8
Bibliography.. 9
Index.. 196

Figures

Figure I... 194

INTRODUCTION

The large published literature contributing to our knowledge of the Late Pleistocene and Holocene climates of North America has been provided by scholars from a number of different disciplines. As a result, it is often difficult for any one worker to be aware of all the published sources of information concerning these climates which exist for a particular geographical area. In recognition of this situation, the following bibliography attempts to facilitate access to these sources. Begun as an attempt to compile and index the literature on North American Holocene climates, coverage was quickly expanded to include immediately pre-Holocene times. Thus, the bibliography, which has been drawn primarily from archaeological, botanical, geological, meteorological, and zoological sources, provides an indexed compilation of the published literature on North American climates of the past 13,000 years.

It is important to note what this bibliography is not. First, it is not an exhaustive bibliography of its subject area. While I hope I have included much, perhaps even most, of the pertinent literature, I certainly have not included all of it. Second, the literature dealing with historic climates as seen through modern instrumental observations is not included. While such studies are of crucial importance to our understanding of past climates, this bibliography is restricted to those studies which deal with periods of time for which modern observational data are not available. Finally, the bibliography does not represent a critical compilation of the literature on North American climates of the past 13,000 years. Included sources range from those which make minor contributions to our understanding of North American paleoclimates to those whose impacts upon this understanding have been considerable. As long as a given study dealt with the subject area it was included; judgments as to the import of the included studies are left to those who use the bibliography.

Each entry in the bibliography has been indexed according to seven geographical subdivisions of the United States and Canada (Figure I). In addition, a "General" category has been provided for those studies which deal with much or all of North America; included here are several topical bibliographies whose contents include, but are not limited to, references on North American paleoclimates. In those instances in which a single publication makes specific contributions to several geographical areas, that publication has been listed under each of the appropriate areas.

Acknowledgements

While many libraries and librarians assisted in locating the sources presented in this bibliography, my deepest thanks go to Mrs. Joan Wolek of the Hamilton College Library for the many services which she and her Interlibrary Loan staff provided. To Mrs. Virginia Meso of the Pacific Northwest Forest and Range Experimental Station Library I owe similar thanks. The financial assistance provided by the Mellon Foundation and by Kirkland College for the completion of this work is also gratefully acknowledged.

Abbe, E. C.
1. 1936 Botanical Results of the Grenfell-Forbes Northern Labrador Expedition, 1931. Rhodora 38: 102-161.

2. 1938 Phytogeographical Observations in Northernmost Labrador. American Geographical Society Special Publications 22: 217-234.

Adam, D. P.
3. 1964 Exploratory Palynology in the Sierra Nevada, California. Geochronology Laboratories, University of Arizona, Interim Research Report 4.

4. 1967 Late-Pleistocene and Recent Palynology in the Central Sierra Nevada, California. In, E. J. Cushing and H. E. Wright, Jr. (eds.), Quaternary Paleoecology, pp. 275-301. Yale University Press, New Haven.

Adams, C. C.
5. 1902 Postglacial Origin and Migration of the Life of Northeastern United States. Journal of Geography 1: 303-310.

Agerter, S. R., and W. S. Glock
6. 1965 An Annotated Bibliography of Tree Growth and Growth Rings, 1950-1962. University of Arizona Press, Tucson.

Ahlmann, H. W.
7. 1953 Glacier Variations and Climatic Fluctuations. American Geographical Society, New York.

Aikens, C. M.
8   1970 Hogup Cave. University of Utah Anthropological Papers 93.

Albanese, J.
9   1973 Geology of the Casper Archaeological Site. Abstracts with Programs 5(7): 530. Geological Society of America.

Albritton, C. C., and K. Bryan
10   1939 Quaternary Stratigraphy in the Davis Mountains, Trans-Pecos Texas. Geological Society of America Bulletin 50: 1423-1474.

Allison, I. S.
11   1945 Pumice Beds at Summer Lake, Oregon. Geological Society of America Bulletin 56: 789-808.

12   1946 Early Man in Oregon. Pluvial Lakes and Pumice. Scientific Monthly 62: 63-65.

13   1949 Wind Erosion Basins in Fort Rock Valley, Oregon. Oregon Academy of Science Proceedings 1: 55.

14   1952 Dating of Pluvial Lakes in the Great Basin. American Journal of Science 250: 907-909.

15   1953 Reply (to Antevs 1953, American Journal of Science). American Journal of Science 251: 237-238.

16   1966 Fossil Lake, Oregon: Its Geology and Fossil Faunas. Oregon State Monographs, Studies in Geology 9. Oregon State University, Corvallis.

Anderson, E.
17   1968 Fauna of the Little Box Elder Cave, Converse County, Wyoming. The Carnivora. University of Colorado Studies, Series in Earth Sciences 6: 1-59.

Anderson, S. T.
18   1954 A Late Glacial Pollen Diagram from Southern Michigan, U. S. A. Danmarks Geologiske Undersogelse (11) 80: 140-155.

Anderson, S. T., and T. P. Bank II
19   1952 Pollen and Radiocarbon Studies of Aleutian Soil Profiles. Science 116: 84-86.

Andrews, J. T.
20   1972 Recent and Fossil Growth Rates of Marine Bivalves, Canadian Arctic, and Late-Quaternary Arctic Marine Environments. Palaeogeography, Palaeoclimatology, Palaeoecology 11: 157-176.

21   1973 The Wisconsin Laurentide Ice Sheet: Dispersal Centers, Problems of Rates of Retreat, and Climatic Implications. Arctic and Alpine Research 5: 185-199.

Andrews, J. T., and R. G. Barry
22   1972 Present and Paleo-Climatic Influences on the Glacierization and Deglacierization of Cumberland Peninsula, Baffin Island, N. W. T., Canada. Institute of Arctic and Alpine Research Occasional Paper 2, Chapter 6. University of Colorado, Boulder.

Andrews, J. T., and J. D. Ives
23   1972 Late- and Postglacial Events (<10,000 BP) in the Eastern Canadian Arctic with Particular Reference to the Cockburn Moraines and Break-up of the Laurentide Ice Sheet. In, Y. Vasari, H. Hyvärinen, and S. Hicks (eds.), Climatic Changes in Arctic Areas during the Last Ten-Thousand Years. <u>Acta Universitatis Ouluensis, Series A: Scientiae Rerum Naturalium 3, Geologica</u> 1: 149-174. University of Oulu, Oulu.

Andrews, J. T., and P. J. Webber
24   1964 A Lichenometrical Study of the Northwestern Margin of the Barnes Ice Cap: A Geomorphological Technique. <u>Geographical Bulletin</u> 22: 80-104.

Andrews, J. T., R. G. Barry, and L. Draper
25   1970 An Inventory of the Present and Past Glacierization of Home Bay and Okoa Bay, East Baffin Island, N. W. T., and some Climatic and Paleoclimatic Considerations. <u>Journal of Glaciology</u> 9: 337-362.

Andrews, J. T., J. T. Buckley, and J. H. England
26   1970 Glacial Chronology and Glacio-Isostatic Recovery, Home Bay, East Baffin Island, Canada. <u>Geological Society of America Bulletin</u> 81: 1123-1148.

Andrews, J. T., et. al.
27   1972 Holocene and Late Glacial Maximum and Marine Transgression in the Eastern Canadian Arctic. <u>Nature (Physical Science)</u> 329: 147-149.

28   1972 Past and Present Glaciological Responses to Climate in Eastern Baffin Island. <u>Quaternary Research</u> 2: 303-314.

29   1973 Holocene Stratigraphy and Geochronology of Four Bogs (3,700 m), San Juan Mountains, SW Colorado, and Implications to the Neoglacial Record. <u>Abstracts with Programs</u> 5: 460-461. Geological Society of America.

Antevs, E.
30   1925 On the Pleistocene History of the Great Basin. In, Quaternary Climates. <u>Carnegie Institute of Washington Publication</u> 352: 51-114.

31   1925 The Big Tree as a Climatic Measure. In, Quaternary Climates. <u>Carnegie Institute of Washington Publication</u> 352: 115-153.

32   1928 The Last Glaciation, with Special Reference to the Ice Retreat in Northeastern North America. <u>American Geographical Society Research Series</u> 17.

33   1931 Late Glacial Correlations and Ice Recession in Manitoba. <u>Geological Survey of Canada Memoir</u> 168.

34   1935 The Occurrence of Flints and Extinct Animals in Pluvial Deposits near Clovis, New Mexico. Part II - Age of the Clovis Lake Clays. <u>Academy of Natural Sciences of Philadelphia Proceedings</u> 87: 304-312.

35   1935 The Spread of Aboriginal Man to North America. <u>Geographical Review</u> 35: 302-309.

36   1936 Correlations of Late Quaternary Chronologies. Sixteenth Geological Congress Report: 213-216.

37   1936 Dating Records of Early Man in the Southwest. American Naturalist 70: 331-336.

38   1936 Pluvial and Postpluvial Fluctuations of Climate in the Southwest. Carnegie Institute of Washington Year-book 35: 322-323.

39   1937 Climate and Early Man in North America. In, G. G. MacCurdy (ed.), Early Man, pp. 125-132. Lippincott, Philadelphia.

40   1938 Postpluvial Climatic Variations in the Southwest. American Meteorological Society Bulletin 19: 190-193.

41   1938 Rainfall and Tree Growth in the Great Basin. Carnegie Institute of Washington Publication 469; American Geographical Society Publication 21.

42   1940 Age of Artifacts below Peat Beds in Lower Klamath Lake, California. Carnegie Institute of Washington Year-book 39: 307-309.

43   1940 Studies in Past Climatic Variations and Their Correlations. Carnegie Institute of Washington Year-book 39: 306-307.

44   1943 Review of "The Boylston Street Fishweir" by F. Johnson, et. al. American Antiquity 8: 304-307.

45   1944 Regarding J. C. Jones' Date for Lake Lahontan. American Antiquity 10: 211.

46   1945 Correlations of Wisconsin Glacial Maxima. American Journal of Science 243-A: 1-39.

47   1946 Review of "Pumice Beds at Summer Lake, Oregon", by I. S. Allison (Geological Society of America Bulletin 56: 789-808). American Antiquity 12: 60-61.

48   1948 Climatic Changes and Pre-White Man. In, The Great Basin with Emphasis on Glacial and Postglacial Times. University of Utah Bulletin 38, Biological Series 10: 168-191.

49   1948 Review of "Patschke Bog". Journal of Geology 56: 83-84.

50   1950 Conditions of Deposition and Erosion by Streams in Dry Regions of the Great Plains. In, J. D. Jennings (ed.), Proceedings of the Sixth Plains Archaeological Conference. University of Utah Anthropological Papers 11: 42-45A.

51   1950 Post Glacial Climatic History of the Great Plains and Dating the Records of Man. In, J. D. Jennings (ed.), Proceedings of the Sixth Plains Archaeological Conference. University of Utah Anthropological Papers 11: 46-51.

52   1950 Reply to Dr. Benjamin H. Burma. In, J. D. Jennings (ed.), Proceedings of the Sixth Plains Archaeological Conference. University of Utah Anthropological Papers 11: 56-59.

53   1951 Climatic History and the Antiquity of Man in California. University of California Archaeological Survey Reports 16: 23-31.

54   1952 Arroyo-Cutting and Filling. Journal of Geology 60: 375-385.

55   1952 Cenozoic Climates of the Great Basin. Geologische Rundschau 40: 94-108.

56   1953 Communication (reply to Allision 1952, American Journal of Science). American Journal of Science 251: 237.

57   1953 Geochronology of the Deglacial and Neothermal Ages. Journal of Geology 61: 195-230.

58   1953 On Divisions of the Last 20,000 Years. University of California Archaeological Survey Reports 22: 5-8.

59   1953 The Post-Pluvial or Neothermal. University of California Archaeological Survey Reports 22: 9-23.

60   1954 Geochronology of the Deglacial and Neothermal Ages: A Reply. Journal of Geology 62: 516-521.

61   1955 Geologic-Climatic Dating in the West. American Antiquity 20: 317-335.

62   1955 Geologic-Climatic Method of Dating. In, T. C. Smiley (ed.), Geochronology. University of Arizona Physical Science Bulletin 2: 151-169.

63   1955 Varve and Radiocarbon Chronologies Appraised by Pollen Data. Journal of Geology 63: 495-499.

64   1957 Geological Tests of the Varve and Radiocarbon Chronologies. Journal of Geology 65: 129-148.

65   1958 Review of "Glacial and Pleistocene Geology" by
      R. F. Flint. American Antiquity 23: 441-442.

66   1959 Geologic Age of the Lehner Mammoth Site. American
      Antiquity 25: 31-34.

67   1962 Late Quaternary Climates in Arizona. American
      Antiquity 28: 193-198.

68   1962 Transatlantic Climatic Agreement Versus C-14
      Dates. Journal of Geology 70: 194-205.

Argus, G. W., and M. B. Davis
69   1962 Macrofossils from a Late-Glacial Deposit at Cambridge,
      Massachusetts. American Midland Naturalist 67: 106-117.

Artist, R. C.
70   1936 Stratigraphy and Preliminary Pollen Analysis of
      a Lake County, Illinois, Bog. Butler University
      Botanical Studies 3: 191-198.

71   1939 Pollen Spectrum Studies on the Anoka Sand Plain
      in Minnesota. Ecological Monographs 9: 493-535.

Aronow, S.
72   1957 On the Postglacial History of the Devils Lake Region,
      North Dakota. Journal of Geology 65: 410-427.

Arthur, G. W.
73   1968 Southern Montana. In, W. W. Caldwell (ed.),
      The Northwestern Plains: A Symposium. The Center
      for Indian Studies, Occasional Paper 1: 51-62. Rocky
      Mountain College, Billings.

Asch, N. B., R. I. Ford, and D. L. Asch
74   1972 Paleoethnobotany of the Koster Site: The Archaic Horizon. Illinois State Museum, Report of Investigations 24; Illinois Valley Archaeological Program Research Papers 6. Illinois State Museum, Springfield.

Aschmann, H. H.
75   1958 Great Basin Climates in Relation to Human Occupance. University of California Archaeological Survey Reports 42: 23-40.

Ashworth, A. C., and J. A. Brophy
76   1972 Late Quaternary Fossil Beetle Assemblage from the Missouri Coteau, North Dakota. Geological Society of America Bulletin 83: 2981-2988.

Ashworth, A. C., L. Clayton, and W. B. Bickley
77   1972 The Mosbeck Site: A Paleoenvironmental Interpretation of the Late Quaternary History of Lake Agassiz Based on Fossil Insect and Mollusk Populations. Quaternary Research 2: 176-188.

Auer, V.
78   1927 Stratigraphic and Morphological Investigations of Peat Bogs of Southeastern Canada. Communicationes ex Instituto Quaestionum Forestalium Finlandiae 12: 1-62.

79   1930 Peat Bogs in Southeastern Canada. Canada Department of Mines, Geological Survey Memoir 162.

80   1933 Peat Bogs in Southeastern Canada. Handbuch der Moorkunde 7: 141-221.

Baerreis, D. A.
81 1967 A Preliminary Analysis of Gastropods from the Mill Creek Sites. In, D. A. Baerreis and R. A. Bryson (eds.), Climatic Change and the Mill Creek Culture of Iowa. Archives of Archaeology 29: 609-632. Society for American Archaeology.

Baerreis, D. A., and R. A. Bryson
82 1965 Climatic Episodes and the Dating of the Mississippi Cultures. Wisconsin Archeologist 46: 203-220.

83 1965 Historical Climatology and the Southern Plains: A Preliminary Statement. Oklahoma Anthropological Society Bulletin 13: 69-75.

84 1966 Dating the Panhandle Aspect Cultures. Oklahoma Anthropological Society Bulletin 14: 105-116.

Baerreis, D. A., and R. A. Bryson (eds.)
85 1967 Climatic Change and the Mill Creek Culture of Iowa. Archives of Archaeology 29. Society for American Archaeology.

Bailey, R. E.
86 1966 Postglacial Pollen Sequence in a Bog of the Loesell Field Laboratory of Eastern Michigan University. Michigan Academy of Science Papers 51: 167-174.

Baker, F. C.
87 1969 The Life of the Pleistocene or Glacial Period. AMS Press, New York (reprint of University of Illinois Museum of Natural History Contributions 7, 1920).

Baker, R. G.
88   1965 Late-Glacial Pollen and Plant Macrofossils from Spider Creek, Southern St. Louis County, Minnesota. Geological Society of America Bulletin 76: 601-610.

89   1970 A Radiocarbon-Dated Pollen Sequence for Wisconsin: Disterhaft Farm Bog Revisited. Abstracts with Programs 2(7): 488. Geological Society of America.

90   1970 Pollen Sequence from Late Quaternary Sediments in Yellowstone Park. Science 168: 1449-1450.

Baldwin, D.
91   1970 Bird Feathers from Hogup Cave. In, C. M. Aikens, Hogup Cave. University of Utah Anthropological Papers 93: 267-269.

Baldwin, G. C.
92   1935 Ring Record of the Great Drought (1276-1299) in Eastern Arizona. Tree-Ring Bulletin 2: 11-12.

Barendson, G. W., E. S. Deevey, Jr., and L. J. Gralenski
93   1957 Yale Natural Radiocarbon Measurements. Science 126: 909-919.

Barghoorn, E. S.
94   1949 Paleobotanical Deposits of the Fishweir and Associated Deposits. In, F. Johnson (ed.), The Boylston Street Fishweir II. Papers of the R. S. Peabody Foundation for Archaeology 4(1): 49-83.

Barnett, J.
95   1937 Pollen Study of Cranberry Pond, near Emporia, Madison County, Indiana. Butler University Botanical Studies 4: 55-64.

Bartley, D. D., and B. Matthews
96   1969 A Paleobotanical Investigation of Postglacial Deposits in the Sugluk Area of Northern Ungava (Quebec, Canada). Review of Palaeobotany and Palynology 9: 45-61.

Bassett, I. J., and J. Terasmae
97   1962 Ragweeds, Ambrosia Species, in Canada and Their History in Postglacial Times. Canadian Journal of Botany 40: 141-150.

Bateman, P. C., and C. Wahrhaftig
98   1966 Geology of the Sierra Nevada. In, H. E. Bailey (ed.), Geology of Northern California. California Division of Mines and Geology Bulletin 190: 107-172.

Baumhoff, M. A., and R. F. Heizer
99   1965 Postglacial Climates and Archaeology in the Desert West. In, H. E. Wright, Jr., and D. G. Frey (eds.), The Quaternary of the United States, pp. 697-707. Princeton University Press, Princeton.

Beard, J. H.
100   1973 Pleistocene-Holocene Boundary and Wisconsinan Substages, Gulf of Mexico. In, R. F. Black, R. P. Goldthwait, and H. B. Willman (eds.), The Wisconsinan Stage. Geological Society of America Memoir 136: 277-316.

Bedwell, S. F.
101   1971 New Evidence for the Presence of Turkey in the Early Postglacial Period of the Northern Great Basin. Great Basin Naturalist 31: 48-49.

102   1973 Fort Rock Basin: Prehistory and Environment. University of Oregon Press, Eugene.

Bedwell, S. F., and L. S. Cressman
103   1971 Fort Rock Report: Prehistory and Environment of the Pluvial Fort Rock Area of South-Central Oregon. In, C. M. Aikens (ed.), Great Basin Anthropological Conference 1970: Selected Papers. University of Oregon Anthropological Papers 1: 1-26.

Beetham, N., and W. A. Niering
104   1961 A Pollen Diagram from Southeastern Connecticut. American Journal of Science 259: 69-75.

Benedict, J. B.
105   1966 Radiocarbon Dates from a Stone-Banked Terrace in the Colorado Rocky Mountains, U. S. A. Geografiska Annaler 48A: 24-31.

106   1968 Recent Glacial History of an Alpine Area in the Colorado Front Range, U. S. A. II. Dating the Glacial Deposits. Journal of Glaciology 7(49): 77-87.

107   1970 Altithermal Occupation of the Front Range Alpine Region. American Quaternary Association, First Meeting, Abstracts: 8.

108   1973 Chronology of Cirque Glaciation, Colorado Front Range. Quaternary Research 3: 584-599.

Benninghoff, W. S.
109   1942 The Pollen Analysis of the Lower Peat. In, F. Johnson (ed.), The Boylston Street Fishweir. Papers of the R. S. Peabody Foundation for Archaeology 2: 96-104.

110 1950 Late Quaternary Vegetation on No Man's Land Island, Massachusetts. Geological Society of America Bulletin 61: 1443-1444.

111 1954 Quaternary Vegetation of Central Alaska. Eighth International Botanical Congress, Paris, Comptes Rendus, Section 6: 246.

112 1957 Interglacial and Late-Glacial Vegetation of the North-Central U. S. Geological Society of America Bulletin 68: 1888.

113 1961 Review of "Late Pleistocene Environments of North Pacific North America" by C. J. Heusser. Science 133: 1243-1244.

114 1964 The Prairie Peninsula as a Filter Barrier to Postglacial Plant Migration. Indiana Academy of Science Proceedings 73: 116-124.

Benninghoff, W. S., and C. W. Hibbard
115 1961 Fossil Pollen Associated with a Late-Glacial Woodland Musk Ox in Michigan. Papers of the Michigan Academy of Science, Arts and Letters 46: 155-159.

Bennion, G. C., R. K. Vickery, and W. P. Cottam
116 1961 Hybridization of Populus fremontii and Populus angustifolia in Perry Canyon, Box Elder County, Utah. Proceedings of the Utah Academy of Sciences, Arts and Letters 38: 31-35.

Bense, J.
117 1971 Cultural Stability on the Lower Snake River during the Altithermal. In, C. M. Aikens (ed.), Great Basin Anthropological Conference 1970: Selected Papers. University of Oregon Anthropological Papers 1: 37-42.

Bent, A. M., and H. E. Wright, Jr.
118 1963 Pollen Analysis of Surface Materials and Lake Sediments from the Chuska Mountains, New Mexico. Geological Society of America Bulletin 74: 491-500.

Bird, J. B. (ed.)
119 1973 The Wisconsin Deglaciation of Canada. Arctic and Alpine Research 5: 163-238.

Birkeland, P. W.
120 1964 Pleistocene Glaciation of the Northern Sierra Nevada, North of Lake Tahoe, California. Journal of Geology 72: 810-825.

Birkeland, P. W., and C. D. Miller
121 1973 Reinterpretation of the Type Temple Lake Moraine and other Neoglacial Deposits, Southern Wind River Mountains, Wyoming. Abstracts with Programs 5: 465-466. Geological Society of America.

Birman, J. H.
122 1954 Pleistocene Glaciation in the Upper San Joaquin Basin, Sierra Nevada. In, R. H. Jahns (ed.), Geology of Southern California. California Department of Natural Resources Division of Mines Bulletin 170: 41-44.

123 1964 Glacial Geology across the Crest of the Sierra Nevada, California. Geological Society of America Special Paper 75.

Bissell, H. J.
124 1968 Bonneville - An Ice Age Lake. Brigham Young University Geology Studies 15: 1-66.

Black, M., and C. E. Eyman
125   1963 The Union Lake Skull, A Possible Early Indian Find in Michigan. American Antiquity 29: 39-48.

Blackwelder, E.
126   1948 The Geological Background. In, The Great Basin with Emphasis on Glacial and Postglacial Times. University of Utah Bulletin 38, Biological Series 10: 3-16.

Blair, W. F.
127   1965 Amphibian Speciation. In, H. E. Wright, Jr., and D. G. Frey (eds.), The Quaternary of the United States, pp. 543-556. Princeton University Press, Princeton.

Blake, W., Jr.
128   1972 Climatic Implications of Radiocarbon-Dated Driftwood in the Queen Elizabeth Islands, Arctic Canada. In, Y. Vasari, H. Hyvärinen, and S. Hicks (eds.), Climatic Changes in Arctic Areas during the Last Ten-Thousand Years. Acta Universitatis Ouluensis, Series A: Scientiae Rerum Naturalium 3, Geologica 1: 78-104. University of Oulu, Oulu.

Bleakney, J. S.
129   1958 A Zoogeographical Study of the Amphibians and Reptiles of Eastern Canada. National Museum of Canada Bulletin 155.

Bohrer, V. S.
130   1966 Pollen Analysis of the Hay Hollow Site East of Snowflake, Arizona. Geochronology Laboratories, University of Arizona, Interim Research Report 12.

Borchert, J. R.
131 1950 The Climate of the Central North American Grasslands. <u>Annals of the Association of American Geographers</u> 40: 1-39.

Borns, H. W.
132 1970 Late Wisconsin Fluctuations of the Laurentide Ice Sheet in New England. <u>Abstracts with Programs</u> 2(7): 499-500. Geological Society of America.

Borns, H. W., and G. H. Denton
133 1972 Port Huron Readvance in Eastern North America (?). <u>Abstracts with Programs</u> 4(7): 455. Geological Society of America.

Borns, H. W., and R. P. Goldthwait
134 1966 Late-Pleistocene Fluctuations of Kaskawulsh Glacier, Southwestern Yukon Territory. <u>American Journal of Science</u> 264: 600-619.

Bourque, B. J.
135 1973 Aboriginal Settlement and Subsistence on the Maine Coast. <u>Man in the Northeast</u> 6: 3-20.

Bowman, P. W.
136 1931 Study of a Peat-Bog near the Matamek River, Quebec, Canada, by the Method of Pollen Analysis. <u>Ecology</u> 12: 694-708.

137 1934 Pollen Analysis of Kodiak Bogs. <u>Ecology</u> 15: 97-100.

Braun, E. L.
138 1928 Glacial and Post-Glacial Plant Migrations Indicated by Relict Colonies of Southern Ohio. <u>Ecology</u> 9: 284-302.

139   1934 History of Ohio's Vegetation. *Ohio Journal of Science* 34: 247-257.

140   1951 Plant Distribution in Relation to the Glacial Boundary. *Ohio Journal of Science* 51: 139-146.

141   1955 The Phytogeography of Unglaciated Eastern United States and its Interpretation. *Botanical Review* 21: 297-370.

Bray, J. R.
142   1964 Chronology of a Small Glacier in Eastern British Columbia, Canada. *Science* 144: 287-288.

143   1970 Temporal Patterning of Post-Pleistocene Glaciation. *Nature* 228: 353.

Bray, J. R., and G. J. Struik
144   1963 Forest Growth and Glacial Chronology in Eastern British Columbia, and Their Relation to Recent Climatic Trends. *Canadian Journal of Botany* 41: 1245-1271.

Bretz, J. H., and L. Horberg
145   1949 Caliche in Southeastern New Mexico. *Journal of Geology* 57: 491-511.

Bright, R. C.
146   1966 Pollen and Seed Stratigraphy of Swan Lake, Southeastern Idaho: Its Relation to Regional Vegetational History and to Lake Bonneville History. *Tebiwa* 9(2): 1-47.

Broecker, W. S.
147   1957 Evidence for a Major Climatic Change Close to 11,000 B. P. *Geological Society of America Bulletin* 68: 1703-1704.

Broecker, W. S., and W. R. Farrand
148   1963 Radiocarbon Age of the Two Creeks Forest Bed. Geological Society of America Bulletin 75: 795-802.

Broecker, W. S., and A. Kaufman
149   1965 Radiocarbon Chronology of Lake Lahontan and Lake Bonneville II, Great Basin. Geological Society of America Bulletin 76: 537-566.

Broecker, W. S., and P. C. Orr
150   1956 Late Wisconsin History of Lake Lahontan. Geological Society of America Bulletin 67: 1675-1676.

151   1958 The Radiocarbon Chronology of Lake Lahontan and Lake Bonneville. Geological Society of America Bulletin 69: 1009-1032.

Broecker, W. S., and A. F. Walton
152   1959 Re-Evaluation of the Salt Chronology of Several Great Basin Lakes. Geological Society of America Bulletin 70: 601-618.

Broecker, W. S., M. Ewing, and B. C. Heezen
153   1960 Evidence for an Abrupt Change in Climate Close to 11,000 Years Ago. American Journal of Science 258: 429-448.

Bromley, S. W.
154   1935 The Original Forest Types of Southern New England. Ecological Monographs 5: 61-89.

Brooks, C. E. P.
155   1949 Climate through the Ages. Ernst Benn, Limited, London (reprinted by Dover Publications, New York, 1970).

Brooks, H. K.
156 1973 Holocene Climatic Changes in Peninsular Florida. Abstracts with Programs 5(7): 558-559. Geological Society of America.

Brown, J.
157 1965 Radiocarbon Dating, Barrow, Alaska. Arctic 18: 36-48.

Brown, J., and C. Cleland
158 1969 The Late Glacial and Early Postglacial Faunal Resources in Midwestern Biomes Newly Opened to Human Adaptation. In, R. E. Bergstrom (ed.), The Quaternary of Illinois. University of Illinois College of Agriculture Special Publication 14: 114-122.

Brush, G. S.
159 1967 Pollen Analysis of Late-Glacial and Postglacial Sediments in Iowa. In, E. J. Cushing and H. E. Wright, Jr. (eds.), Quaternary Paleoecology, pp. 99-115. Yale University Press, New Haven.

Bryan, A. L., and R. Gruhn
160 1964 Problems Relating to the Neothermal Climatic Sequence. American Antiquity 29: 307-315.

Bryan, K.
161 1926 Recent Deposits of Chaco Canyon, New Mexico, in Relation to the Life of the Prehistoric Peoples of Pueblo Bonito. Washington Academy of Sciences Journal 16: 75-76.

162 1928 Change in Plant Associations by Change in Ground Water Level. Ecology 9: 474-478.

163 1932 Paleoclimatology in North America as a Result of the Study of Peat Bogs. Zeitschrift für Gletscherkunde und Glazialgeologie 20: 76-81.

164 1939 Stone Cultures near Cerro Pedernal and Their Geological Antiquity. Texas Archeological and Paleontological Society Bulletin 11: 9-42.

165 1940 Erosion in the Valleys of the Southwest. New Mexico Quarterly 10: 227-232.

166 1941 Correlation of the Deposits of Sandia Cave, New Mexico, with the Glacial Chronology. In, F. G. Hibben, Evidences of Early Occupation in Sandia Cave and other Sites in the Sandia-Manzano Region. Smithsonian Miscellaneous Collections 99(23): 45-64.

167 1941 Geologic Antiquity of Man in America. Science 93: 505-514.

168 1941 Pre-Columbian Agriculture in the Southwest as Conditioned by Periods of Alluviation. Annals of the Association of American Geographers 31: 219-242.

169 1950 Geological Interpretations of the Deposits. In, E. W. Haury, et. al., The Stratigraphy and Archaeology of Ventana Cave, pp. 75-126. The University of New Mexico and the University of Arizona Presses, Albuquerque and Tucson.

170 1954 The Geology of Chaco Canyon, New Mexico, in Relation to the Life and Remains of the Prehistoric Peoples of Pueblo Bonito. Smithsonian Miscellaneous Collections 122(7): 1-65.

Bryan, K., and C. C. Albritton, Jr.
171 1942 Wind-Polished Rocks in the Trans-Pecos Region, Texas and New Mexico. Geological Society of America Bulletin 53: 1403-1416.

172 1943 Soil Phenomena as Evidence of Climatic Changes. American Journal of Science 241: 469-490.

Bryan, K., and F. T. McCann
173 1943 Sand Dunes and Alluvium near Grants, New Mexico. American Antiquity 8: 281-295.

Bryan, K., and L. L. Ray
174 1940 Geologic Antiquity of the Lindenmeier Site in Colorado. Smithsonian Miscellaneous Collections 99(2).

Bryant, V. M., and R. K. Holz
175 1968 The Role of Pollen in the Reconstruction of Past Environments. The Pennsylvania Geographer 6: 11-19.

Bryant, V. M., and D. A. Larsen
176 1968 Pollen Analysis of the Devil's Mouth Site, Val Verde County, Texas. In, W. M. Sorrow, The Devil's Mouth Site: The Third Season - 1967. Texas Archaeological Salvage Project Papers 14: 57-70.

Bryson, R. A.
177 1966 Air Masses, Streamlines, and the Boreal Forest. Geographical Bulletin 8: 228-269.

178 1970 The Character of Climatic Change, and the End of the Pleistocene. American Quaternary Association, First Meeting, Abstracts: 20-22.

Bryson, R. A., and D. A. Baerreis
179   1967 Introduction and Project Summary. In, D. A. Baerreis and R. A. Bryson (eds.), Climatic Change and the Mill Creek Culture of Iowa. Archives of Archaeology 29: 1-61. Society for American Archaeology.

Bryson, R. A., and P. Julian (eds.)
180   1963 Proceedings of the Conference on the Climate of the Eleventh and Sixteenth Centuries. National Center for Atmospheric Research, Technical Notes 63-1. Boulder.

Bryson, R. A., and W. M. Wendland
181   1967 Tentative Climatic Patterns for some Late-Glacial and Post-Glacial Episodes in Central North America. In, W. J. Mayer-Oakes (ed.), Life, Land, and Water, pp. 271-298. University of Manitoba Press, Winnipeg.

Bryson, R. A., D. A. Baerreis, and W. M. Wendland
182   1970 The Character of Late-Glacial and Post-Glacial Climatic Changes. In, W. Dort, Jr., and J. K. Jones, Jr. (eds.), Pleistocene and Recent Environments of the Central Great Plains. Department of Geology, University of Kansas, Special Publication 3: 53-74.

Bryson, R. A., W. N. Irving, and J. A. Larsen
183   1965 Radiocarbon and Soil Evidence of Former Forest in the Southern Canadian Tundra. Science 147: 46-48.

Bryson, R. A., et. al.
184   1969 Radiocarbon Isotopes on the Disintegration of the Laurentide Ice Sheet. Arctic and Alpine Research 1: 1-14.

Burma, B. H.
185   1950 Erosion and Sedimentation in the Great Plains: A Criticism of Dr. Antevs' Conference Papers. In, J. D. Jennings (ed.), Proceedings in the Sixth Plains Archaeological Conference. University of Utah Anthropological Papers 11: 52-55.

Burns, G. W.
186   1958 Wisconsin Age Forests in Western Ohio. II. Vegetation and Burial Conditions. Ohio Journal of Science 58: 220-230.

Butler, B. R.
187   1968 An Introduction to Archaeological Investigations in the Pioneer Basin Locality of Eastern Idaho. Tebiwa 11(1): 1-30.

188   1969 More Information on the Frozen Ground Features and Further Interpretations of the Small Mammal Sequence at the Wasden Site (Owl Cave), Bonneville County, Idaho. Tebiwa 12(1): 58-63.

189   1971 The Origin of the Upper Snake Country Buffalo. Tebiwa 14(2): 1-20.

190   1972 The Holocene in the Desert West and its Cultural Significance. In, D. D. Fowler (ed.), Great Basin Cultural Ecology: A Symposium. Desert Research Institute Publications in the Social Sciences 8: 5-12. University of Nevada, Reno.

191   1972 The Holocene or Postglacial Ecological Crisis on the Eastern Snake River Plain. Tebiwa 15(1): 49-64.

192   1973 Folsom and Plano Points from the Peripheries of the Upper Snake Country. Tebiwa 16(1): 69-72.

Butler, P.
193   1959 Palynological Studies of the Barnstable Marsh, Cape Cod, Massachusetts. Ecology 40: 735-737.

Butzer, K. W.
194   1974 Review of "Pleistocene and Recent Environments of the Central Great Plains", W. Dort, Jr., and J. K. Jones, Jr. (eds.), Department of Geology, University of Kansas, Special Publication 3. American Antiquity 39: 398-399.

Byers, D.
195   1946 The Environment of the Northeast. In, F. Johnson (ed.), Man in Northeastern North America. Papers of the R. S. Peabody Foundation for Archaeology 3: 3-32.

Cain, S. A.
196   1939 Pollen Analysis as a Paleo-Ecological Research Method. Botanical Review 5: 627-654.

197   1943 A Note on "Fossil Evidence of Wider Post-Pleistocene Range for Butternut and Hickory in Wisconsin". Rhodora 45: 107-109.

198   1944 Pollen Analysis of some Buried Soils, Spartanburg County, South Carolina. Bulletin of the Torrey Botanical Club 71: 11-22.

Cain, S. A., and L. G. Cain
199   1948 Palynological Studies at Sodon Lake. II. Size-Frequency Studies of Pine Pollen, Fossil and Modern. American Journal of Botany 35: 583-591.

Cain, S. A., and J. V. Slater
200   1948 Palynological Studies at Sodon Lake, Michigan. III. The Sequence of Pollen Spectra, Profile I. Ecology 29: 492-500.

Cain, S. A., L. G. Cain, and G. Thompson
201 1951 Fossil Pine Pollen Size - Frequencies in Heart Lake Sediments, Oakland County, Michigan. American Journal of Botany 38: 724-731.

Cain, S. A., F. Segadas-Vianna, and F. Bunt
202 1950 Mollusks of Sodon Lake, Oakland County, Michigan. I. Stratigraphic Occurrence of Shells in Peat and Marl Sediments. Ecology 31: 540-545.

Calkin, P. E., and J. H. McAndrews
203 1969 Dating Late Glacial Recession and Vegetation in the Erie Basin, North-Western New York. Abstracts with Programs for 1969, Part 1:5. Geological Society of America.

Carrara, P. E., and J. T. Andrews
204 1972 The Quaternary History of Northern Cumberland Peninsula, Baffin Island, N. W. T., Canada. Part I: The Late- and Neoglacial Deposits of the Akudlermuit and Boas Glaciers. Canadian Journal of Earth Sciences 9: 403-414.

205 1973 Holocene Deposits in the Alpine of the San Juan Mountains, S. W. Colorado. Abstracts with Programs 5: 469-470. Geological Society of America.

Cermak, V.
206 1971 Underground Temperatures and Inferred Climatic Temperatures of the Past Millenium. Palaeogeography, Palaeoclimatology, Palaeoecology 10: 1-19.

Cheatum, E. P., and D. Allen
207   1963 An Ecological Comparison of the Ben Franklin and Clear Creek Local Molluscan Faunas in Texas. <u>Southern Methodist University Graduate Research Center Journal</u> 31: 174-179.

208   1966 Ecological Significance of the Fossil Freshwater and Land Shells from the Domebo Mammoth Kill Site. In, F. Leonhardy (ed.), Domebo: A Paleo-Indian Mammoth Kill in the Prairie-Plains. <u>Contributions of the Museum of the Great Plains</u> I: 36-43. Lawton.

Cheney, L. S.
209   1930 Wisconsin Fossil Mosses. <u>Bryologist</u> 33: 66-68.

210   1931 More Fossil Mosses from Wisconsin. <u>Bryologist</u> 34: 93-94.

Cleland, C. E.
211   1965 Barren Ground Caribou <u>Rangifer arcticus</u> from an Early Man Site in Southeastern Michigan. <u>American Antiquity</u> 30: 350-351.

212   1966 The Prehistoric Animal Ecology and Ethnozoology of the Upper Great Lakes Region. <u>Museum of Anthropology, University of Michigan, Anthropological Papers</u> 29.

Clewlow, C. W., Jr., and R. Ambro
213   1972 The Grass Valley Archaeological Project: An Introduction. In, C. W. Clewlow, Jr., and M. Rusco (eds.), The Grass Valley Archaeological Project: Collected Papers. <u>Nevada Archeological Survey Research Paper</u> 3: 1-10. University of Nevada, Reno.

Clisby, K. H., and P. B. Sears
214   1956 San Augustin Plains - Pleistocene Climatic Changes. Science 124: 537-539.

Clisby, K. H., F. Foreman, and P. B. Sears
215   1957 Pleistocene Climatic Changes in New Mexico, U. S. A. Veröffentlichungen des Geobotanischen Instituts, Eidgenössiche Technische Hochschule Rübel in Zürich 34: 21-26.

Cocke, E. C., I. F. Lewis, and R. Patrick
216   1934 A Further Study of Dismal Swamp Peat. American Journal of Botany 21: 374-395.

Colbert, E. H.
217   1950 The Fossil Vertebrates. In, E. W. Haury, et. al., The Stratigraphy and Archaeology of Ventana Cave, Arizona, pp. 126-148. The University of New Mexico and the University of Arizona Presses, Albuquerque and Tucson.

Colinvaux, P. A.
218   1963 A Pollen Record from Arctic Alaska Reaching Glacial and Bering Land Bridge Times. Nature 198: 609-610.

219   1964 Origin of Ice Ages: Pollen Evidence from Arctic Alaska. Science 145: 707-708.

220   1964 The Environment of the Bering Land Bridge. Ecological Monographs 34: 297-329.

221   1965 Pollen from Alaska and the Origin of Ice Ages. Science 147: 633.

222   1966 Quaternary Vegetational History of Arctic Alaska. In, D. M. Hopkins (ed.), <u>The Bering Land Bridge</u>, pp. 207-231. Stanford University Press, Palo Alto.

223   1967 A Long Pollen Record from St. Lawrence Island, Bering Sea (Alaska). <u>Palaeogeography, Palaeoclimatology, Palaeoecology</u> 3: 29-48.

Conant, R.
224   1960 The Queen Snake, <u>Natrix septemvittata</u>, in the Interior Highlands of Arkansas and Missouri, with Comments upon Similar Disjunct Distributions. <u>Academy of Natural Sciences of Philadelphia Proceedings</u> 112: 25-40.

Conant, R., E. S. Thomas, and R. L. Rausch
225   1945 The Plains Garter Snake, <u>Thamnophis radix</u>, in Ohio. <u>Copeia</u> 1945: 61-68.

Conger, P. S.
226   1949 The Diatoms. In, F. Johnson (ed.), The Boylston Street Fishweir II. <u>Papers of the R. S. Peabody Foundation for Archaeology</u> 4(1): 109-123.

Connally, G. G., and L. A. Sirkin
227   1967 The Pleistocene Geology of the Walkill Valley. In, R. H. Waines (ed.), <u>New York State Geological Association, Thirty Ninth Annual Meeting, Guidebook</u>, pp. A1-A16.

228   1970 Late Glacial History of the Upper Walkill Valley, New York. <u>Geological Society of America Bulletin</u> 81: 3297-3306.

229   1971 Luzerne Readvance near Glens Falls, New York. <u>Geological Society of America Bulletin</u> 82: 989-1008.

230 1973 Wisconsinan History of the Hudson-Champlain Lobe. In, R. F. Black, R. P. Goldthwait, and H. B. Willman (eds.), The Wisconsinan Stage. Geological Society of America Memoir 136: 47-69.

Conner, S. W.
231 1968 The Northwestern Plains: An Introduction. In, W. W. Caldwell (ed.), The Northwestern Plains: A Symposium. The Center for Indian Studies, Occasional Paper 1: 13-20. Rocky Mountain College, Billings.

Cooley, M. E.
232 1962 Late Pleistocene and Recent Erosion and Alluviation in Parts of the Colorado River System, Arizona and Utah. United States Geological Survey Professional Paper 450-B: 48-50.

Cooper, W. S.
233 1923 The Recent Ecological History of Glacier Bay, Alaska: I. The Interglacial Forests of Glacier Bay. Ecology 4: 93-128.

234 1931 A Third Expedition to Glacier Bay, Alaska. Ecology 12: 61-95.

235 1935 The History of the Upper Mississippi River in Late Wisconsin and Postglacial Times. Minnesota Geological Survey Bulletin 26.

236 1937 The Problem of Glacier Bay, Alaska: A Study of Glacier Variations. Geographical Review 27: 37-62.

237   1938 Ancient Dunes of the Upper Mississippi Valley as Possible Climatic Indicators. American Meteorological Society Bulletin 19: 193-204.

238   1939 Fourth Expedition to Glacier Bay, Alaska. Ecology 20: 130-155.

239   1942 An Isolated Colony of Plants on a Glacier-Clad Mountain. Bulletin of the Torrey Botanical Club 69: 429-433.

240   1942 Contributions of Botanical Science to the Knowledge of Postglacial Climates. Journal of Geology 50: 981-994.

241   1942 The Vegetation of the Prince William Sound Region, Alaska: with a Brief Excursion into Postglacial Climatic History. Ecological Monographs 12: 1-22.

242   1958 Terminology of Post-Valders Time. Geological Society of America Bulletin 69: 941-945.

Cooper, W. S., and H. Foot
243   1932 Reconstruction of a Late Pleistocene Biotic Community in Minneapolis, Minnesota. Ecology 13: 63-72.

Cottam, W. P., J. M. Tucker, and R. Drobnick
244   1959 Some Clues to Great Basin Postpluvial Climates Provided by Oak Distribution. Ecology 40: 361-377.

Cox, D. D.
245   1959 Some Postglacial Forests in Central and Eastern New York as Determined by the Method of Pollen Analysis. New York State Museum and Science Service Bulletin 377.

246   1968 A Late-Glacial Pollen Record from the West Virginia-Maryland Border. Castanea 33: 137-149.

Cox, D. D., and D. M. Lewis
247   1965 Pollen Studies in the Crusoe Lake Area of Prehistoric Indian Occupation. New York State Museum and Science Service Bulletin 397.

Craig, A. J.
248   1969 Vegetational History of the Shenendoah Valley, Virginia. Geological Society of America Special Paper 123: 283-296.

249   1972 Pollen Influx to Laminated Sediments: A Pollen Diagram from Northeastern Minnesota. Ecology 53: 46-57.

Craig, B. G.
250   1959 Pingo in the Thelon Valley, Northwest Territories; Radiocarbon Age and Historical Significance of the Contained Organic Material. Geological Society of America Bulletin 79: 509-510.

Crandell, D. R.
251   1965 Alpine Glaciers at Mount Rainier, Washington, during Late Pleistocene and Recent Time. Geological Society of America Special Paper 82 (Abstracts for 1964): 34-35.

252   1965 The Glacial History of Western Washington and Oregon. In, H. E. Wright, Jr., and D. G. Frey (eds.), The Quaternary of the United States, pp. 341-353. Princeton University Press, Princeton.

Crandell, D. R., and R. D. Miller
253   1964 Post-Hypsithermal Glacier Advances at Mt. Rainier, Washington. United States Geological Survey Professional Paper 501-D: D110-D114.

Crary, A. P.
254   1960 Arctic Ice Island and Ice Shelf Studies. Arctic 13: 32-50.

Cressman, L. S.
255   1940 Studies on Early Man in South Central Oregon. Carnegie Institute of Washington Year-Book 39: 300-306.

256   1942 Archaeological Researches in the Northern Great Basin. Carnegie Institute of Washington Publication 538.

257   1946 Early Man in Oregon. Stratigraphic Evidence. Scientific Monthly 62: 43-51.

Crook, W. W., Jr.
258   1952 The Wheeler Site: A 3,500 Year-Old Culture in Dallas County, Texas. Field and Laboratory 20: 43-65.

Culberson, W. L.
259   1955 The Fossil Mosses of the Two Creeks Forest Bed of Wisconsin. American Midland Naturalist 54: 452-459.

Curry, R. R.
260   1969 Holocene Climatic and Glacial History of the Central Sierra Nevada, California. Geological Society of America Special Paper 123: 1-47.

261 1971 Glacial and Pleistocene History of the Mammoth Lakes Sierra - A Geologic Guidebook. University of Montana Department of Geology, Geological Series Publication 11.

Curtis, J. T.
262 1959 Postglacial History. In, The Vegetation of Wisconsin, Chapter 22. University of Wisconsin Press, Madison.

Cushing, E. J.
263 1964 Redeposited Pollen in Late-Wisconsin Pollen Spectra from East-Central Minnesota. American Journal of Science 262: 1075-1088.

264 1965 Problems in the Quaternary Phytogeography of the Great Lakes Region. In, H. E. Wright, Jr., and D. G. Frey (eds.), The Quaternary of the United States, pp. 403-416. Princeton University Press, Princeton.

265 1967 Late-Wisconsin Pollen Stratigraphy and the Glacial Sequence in Minnesota. In, E. J. Cushing and H. E. Wright, Jr. (eds.), Quaternary Paleoecology, pp. 59-88. Yale University Press, New Haven.

Cvancara, A. M., et al.
266 1971 Paleolimnology of Late Quaternary Deposits: Siebold Site, North Dakota. Science 171: 172-174.

Dachnowski, A. P.
267 1921 Peat Deposits and Their Evidence of Climatic Changes. Botanical Gazette 72: 57-89.

268 1922 The Correlation of Time Units and Climatic Changes in Peat Deposits of the United States and Europe. Proceedings of the National Academy of Sciences 8: 225-231.

269   1925 Profiles of Peatlands within Limits of Extinct Glacial Lakes Agassiz and Wisconsin. Botanical Gazette 80: 345-366.

270   1926 Profiles of Peat Deposits in New England. Ecology 7: 120-135.

Dachnowski-Stokes, A. P.
271   1929 Records of Climatic Cycles in Peat Deposits. Carnegie Institute of Washington, Reports of the Conferences on Cycles: 55-64.

272   1929 The Botanical Composition and Morphological Features of "Highmoor" Peat Profiles in Maine. Soil Science 27: 379-388.

273   1930 Peat Profile Studies in Maine: The South Lubec Heath in Relation to Sea Level. Washington Academy of Sciences Journal 20: 124-135.

Daily, F. K.
274   1961 Glacial and Post-Glacial Charophytes from New York and Indiana. Butler University Botanical Studies 14: 39-72.

Dansereau, P.
275   1953 The Postglacial Pine Period. Royal Society of Canada Transactions, Series 3, Section 5 47: 23-38.

276   1968 Alpine Vegetation in Eastern North America. Cranbrook Institute of Science Newsletter 37(8): 94-102.

Danson, E. B.
277   1957 Review of "Higgins Flat Pueblo, Western New Mexico" by P. S. Martin, et. al. American Antiquity 23: 201-202.

Darlington, C. H.
278   1943 Vegetation and Substrate of Cranberry Glades, West Virginia. Botanical Gazette 104: 371-393.

Darrow, R. A.
279   1961 Origin and Development of the Vegetational Communities of the Southwest. In, L. M. Shields and L. J. Gardner (eds.), Bioecology of the Arid and Semi-Arid Lands of the Southwest. New Mexico Highlands University Bulletin 212: 30-47.

Daugherty, H. E.
280   1968 Quaternary Climatology of North America with Emphasis on the State of Illinois. In, R. E. Bergstrom (ed.), The Quaternary of Illinois. University of Illinois College of Agriculture Special Publication 14: 61-69.

Daugherty, R. D., et. al.
281   1956 Archaeology of the Lind Coulee Site, Washington. Proceedings of the American Philosophical Society 100(3): 223-278.

Davis, E. L.
282   1967 Man and Water at Pleistocene Lake Mohave. American Antiquity 32: 345-353.

Davis, E. M.
283   1962 Archaeology of the Lime Creek Site in Southwestern Nebraska. University of Nebraska Special Publication 3.

Davis, J. H., Jr.
284   1964 The Peat Deposits of Florida. Their Occurrence, Development, and Uses. Florida Geological Survey Bulletin 30.

Davis, J. O., and R. Elston
285   1972 New Stratigraphic Evidence of Late Quaternary Climatic Change in Northwestern Nevada. In, D. D. Fowler (ed.), Great Basin Cultural Ecology: A Symposium. Desert Research Institute Publications in the Social Sciences 8: 43-55. University of Nevada, Reno.

Davis, M. B.
286   1958 Three Pollen Diagrams from Central Massachusetts. American Journal of Science 256: 540-570.

287   1960 A Late-Glacial Pollen Diagram from Taunton, Massachusetts. Bulletin of the Torrey Botanical Club 87: 258-270.

288   1961 Pollen Diagrams as Evidence of Late-Glacial Climatic Change in Southern New England. New York Academy of Sciences Annals 95: 623-631.

289   1961 The Problem of Rebedded Pollen in Late-Glacial Sediments at Taunton, Massachusetts. American Journal of Science 259: 211-222.

290   1963 On the Theory of Pollen Analysis. American Journal of Science 261: 897-912.

291   1965 Phytogeography and Palynology of Northeastern United States. In, H. E. Wright, Jr., and D. G. Frey (eds.), The Quaternary of the United States, pp. 377-401. Princeton University Press, Princeton.

292   1966 Pollen-Accumulation Rates in Sediment from Rogers Lake, Connecticut. Geological Society of America Special Paper 101 (Abstracts for 1966): 50-51.

293   1967 Late-Glacial Climate in the Northern United States: A Comparison of New England and the Great Lakes Region. In, E. J. Cushing and H. E. Wright, Jr. (eds.), Quaternary Paleoecology, pp. 11-43. Yale University Press, New Haven.

294   1967 Pollen Accumulation Rates at Rogers Lake, Connecticut, during Late- and Postglacial Time. Review of Palaeobotany and Palynology 2: 219-230.

295   1969 Climatic Change in Southern Connecticut Recorded by Pollen Deposition at Rogers Lake. Ecology 50: 409-421.

296   1969 Palynology and Environmental History during the Quaternary Period. American Scientist 57: 317-332.

Davis, M. B., and E. S. Deevey, Jr.
297   1964 Pollen Accumulation Rates: Estimates from Late-Glacial Sediments of Rogers Lake. Science 145: 1293-1295.

Davis, W. A.
298   1966 Theoretical Problems in Western Prehistory. In, W. d'Azevedo, et. al. (eds.), The Current Status of Anthropological Research in the Great Basin, 1964. Desert Research Institute Social Sciences and Humanities Publications 1: 147-165. University of Nevada, Reno.

Dean, J. S.
299   1969 Chronological Analysis of Tsegi Phase Sites in Northeastern Arizona. Papers of the Laboratory of Tree-Ring Research 3.

Deevey, E. S., Jr.

300 1939 Studies on Connecticut Lake Sediments: I. A Postglacial Chronology for Southern New England. American Journal of Science 237: 691-724.

301 1942 Studies on Connecticut Lake Sediments. III. The Biostratonomy of Linsley Pond. American Journal of Science 240: 233-264; 313-324.

302 1943 Additional Pollen Analyses from Southern New England. American Journal of Science 241: 717-752.

303 1944 Pollen Analysis and History. American Scientist 32: 39-53.

304 1944 Pollen Analysis and Mexican Archaeology: An Attempt to Apply the Method. American Antiquity 10: 135-149.

305 1948 On the Date of the Last Rise of Sea Level in Southern New England, with Remarks on the Grassy Island Site. American Journal of Science 246: 329-352.

306 1948 Review of Hansen (1947). Geographical Review 38: 345-347.

307 1949 Biogeography of the Pleistocene. Geological Society of America Bulletin 60: 1315-1416.

308 1951 Late-Glacial and Postglacial Pollen Diagrams from Maine. American Journal of Science 249: 177-207.

309 1953 Paleolimnology and Climate. In, H. Shaplow (ed.), Climatic Change, pp. 273-318. Harvard University Press, Cambridge.

310 1958 Radiocarbon-Dated Pollen Sequences in Eastern North America. Veröffentlichungen des Geobotanischen Instituts, Eidgenössiche Technische Hochschule Rübel in Zürich 34: 30-37.

311 1961 Recent Advances in Pleistocene Stratigraphy and Biogeography. In, W. F. Blair (ed.), Vertebrate Speciation, pp. 594-623. University of Texas Press, Austin.

312 1965 Pleistocene Nonmarine Environments. In, H. E. Wright, Jr., and D. G. Frey (eds.), The Quaternary of the United States, pp. 643-652. Princeton University Press, Princeton.

313 1967 Introduction. In, P. S. Martin and H. E. Wright, Jr. (eds), Pleistocene Extinctions, pp. 63-72. Yale University Press, New Haven.

Deevey, E. S., Jr., and R. F. Flint
314 1957 Postglacial Hypsithermal Interval. Science 125: 182-184.

Deevey, E. S., Jr., and J. E. Potzger
315 1951 Peat Samples for Radio-carbon Analysis: Problems in Pollen Statistics. American Journal of Science 249: 473-511.

Deevey, E. S., Jr., et al.
316 1959 Yale Natural Radiocarbon Measurements IV. American Journal of Science Radiocarbon Supplement 1: 144-172.

Dekin, A. A., Jr.
317 1972 Climatic Change and Cultural Change: A Correlative Study from Eastern Arctic Prehistory. Polar Notes 12: 11-31.

Delisio, M. P.
318   1971 Preliminary Report on the Weston Canyon Rockshelter, Southeastern Idaho: A Big Game Hunting Site in the Northern Great Basin. In, C. M. Aikens (ed.), Great Basin Anthropological Conference, 1970 Selected Papers. University of Oregon Anthropological Papers 1: 43-58.

Denton, G. H.
319   1972 Holocene Glacier Fluctuations and Their Possible Causes. Abstracts with Programs 4(7): 487. Geological Society of America.

Denton, G. H., and W. Karlen
320   1973 Holocene Climatic Fluctuations - Their Pattern and Possible Cause. Quaternary Research 3: 155-205.

Denton, G. H., and S. C. Porter
321   1970 Neoglaciation. Scientific American 222: 101-110.

Denton, G. H., and M. Stuiver
322   1966 Neoglacial Chronology, Northeastern St. Elias Mountains, Canada. American Journal of Science 264: 577-599.

Detling, L. E.
323   1961 The Chapparal Formation of Southwestern Oregon, with Consideration of its Postglacial History. Ecology 42: 348-357.

Detterman, R. L.
324   1953 Sagavanirktok-Anaktuvuk Region, Northern Alaska. In, T. L. Péwé et. al., Multiple Glaciation in Alaska. United States Geological Survey Circular 289: 11-12.

325 1970 Early Holocene Warm Interval in Northern Alaska. Arctic 23: 130-132.

Detterman, R. L., A. L. Bowsher, and J. T. Dutro, Jr.
326 1958 Glaciation on the Arctic Slope of the Brooks Range, Northern Alaska. Arctic 11: 43-61.

Dillon, L. S.
327 1956 Wisconsin Climate and Life Zones in North America. Science 123: 167-176.

Donner, J. J.
328 1964 Pleistocene Geology of Eastern Long Island, New York. American Journal of Science 262: 355-376.

Dorf, E.
329 1959 Climatic Changes of the Past and Present. University of Michigan Museum of Paleontology Contributions 13(8): 181-210.

330 1960 Climatic Changes of the Past and Present. American Scientist 48: 341-364.

Dort, W., Jr.
331 1960 Multiple Glaciation, East Side of Lemhi Range, Idaho. Geological Society of America Bulletin 71: 1852.

332 1962 Multiple Glaciation of Southern Lemhi Mountains, Idaho - Preliminary Reconnaisance Report. Tebiwa 5(2): 2-17.

333 1964 Geology of the Midvale Site Complex, Idaho. Tebiwa 7(1): 17-21.

334   1965 Glaciation in Idaho - A Summary of Present Knowledge. Tebiwa 8(1): 29-36.

335   1968 Paleoclimatic Implications of Soil Structures at the Wasden Site (Owl Cave). Tebiwa 11(1): 31-36.

336   1969 Geologic Evidence of Late-Glacial Recurrent Climatic Fluctuations, Southeastern Idaho. Abstracts with Programs for 1969, Part 7: 50. Geological Society of America.

337   1970 Recurrent Climatic Stress on Pleistocene and Recent Environments. In, W. Dort, Jr., and J. K. Jones, Jr. (eds.), Pleistocene and Recent Environments of the Central Great Plains. Department of Geology, University of Kansas, Special Publication 3: 3-7.

Dort, W., Jr., and J. K. Jones, Jr. (eds.)
338   1970 Pleistocene and Recent Environments of the Central Great Plains. Department of Geology, University of Kansas, Special Publication 3.

Douglass, A. E.
339   1919 Climatic Cycles and Tree Growth. A Study of the Annual Rings of Trees in Relation to Climate and Solar Activity. Carnegie Institute of Washington Publication 289, Volume I.

340   1928 Climatic Cycles and Tree Growth. Volume II. A Study of the Annual Rings of Trees in Relation to Climate and Solar Activity. Carnegie Institute of Washington Publication 289, Volume II.

341   1929 The Secret of the Southwest Solved by Talkative Tree Rings. National Geographic 56: 737-770.

342   1933 Evidences of Cycles in Tree-Ring Records. Proceedings of the National Academy of Sciences 19: 350-360.

343   1933 Tree Growth and Climatic Cycles. Scientific Monthly 37: 481-495.

344   1935 Dating Pueblo Bonito and other Ruins of the Southwest. National Geographic Society Contributed Technical Papers, Pueblo Bonito Series I.

345   1936 Climatic Cycles and Tree Growth. Volume III. A Study of Cycles. Carnegie Institute of Washington Publication 289, Volume III.

Douglas, L. A., and J. C. F. Tedrow
346   1960 Tundra Soils of Arctic Alaska. Seventh International Congress of Soil Science Transactions 4: 291-304.

Draper, P. I.
347   1928 A Demonstration of the Technique of Pollen Analysis. Oklahoma Academy of Science Proceedings 8: 63-64.

348   1929 A Comparison of Pollen Spectra of Old and Young Bogs in the Erie Basin. Oklahoma Academy of Science Proceedings 9: 50-53.

Dreimanis, A.
349   1953 Two Late Wisconsin Interstadial Deposits from Ontario, Canada. Geological Society of America Bulletin 64: 1414.

350   1967 Mastodons, Their Geologic Age and Extinction in Ontario, Canada. Canadian Journal of Earth Sciences 4: 663-675.

351   1968 Extinction of Mastodons in Eastern North America; Testing a New Climatic-Environmental Hypothesis. Ohio Journal of Science 68: 257-272.

Dreimanis, A., and P. F. Karrow
352   1973 Glacial History of the Great Lakes - St. Lawrence Region, the Classification of the Wisconsin(an) Stage and its Correlatives. Twenty Fourth International Geological Congress, Section 12: 5-15.

Duffield, L. F.
353   1974 Nonhuman Vertebrate Remains from Salts Cave Vestibule. In, P. J. Watson (ed.), Archeology of the Mammoth Cave Area, pp. 123-133. Academic Press, New York.

Durkee, L. H.
354   1961 Pollen Profiles from Five Bog Lakes in New York State. Dissertation Abstracts 21: 2446-2447.

Durrant, S. D.
355   1970 Faunal Remains as Indicators of Neothermal Climates at Hogup Cave. In, C. M. Aikens, Hogup Cave. University of Utah Anthropological Papers 93: 241-245.

Dyck, W., et. al.
356   1966 Geological Survey of Canada Radiocarbon Dates. V. Radiocarbon 8: 96-127.

Eardley, A. J.
357   1962 Gypsum Dunes and Evaporite History of the Great Salt Lake Desert. Utah Geological and Mineralogical Survey Special Studies 2.

Eardley, A. J., and V. Gvodetsky
358   1960 Analysis of Pleistocene Core from Great Salt Lake, Utah. Geological Society of America Bulletin 71: 1323-1344.

Eardley, A. J., V. Gvodetsky, and R. E. Marsell
359   1957 Hydrology of Lake Bonneville and Sediments and Soils of its Basin. Geological Society of America Bulletin 68: 1141-1202.

Eddy, S., and A. E. Jenks
360   1935 A Kitchen Midden with Bones of Extinct Animals in the Upper Lakes Area. Science 81: 535.

Eisely, L. C.
361   1937 Index Mollusca and Their Bearing on Certain Problems of Prehistory: A Critique. In, D. S. Davidson (ed.), Twenty-Fifth Anniversary Studies. Philadelphia Anthropological Society Publications 1: 77-93.

362   1939 Pollen Analysis and its Bearing upon American Prehistory: A Critique. American Antiquity 5: 115-139.

Elston, R. G.
363   1971 A Contribution to Washo Archaeology. Nevada Archeological Survey Research Paper 2. University of Nevada, Reno.

Emery, K. O., R. C. Wigley, and M. Rubin
364   1965 A Submerged Peat Deposit off the Atlantic Coast of the United States. *Limnology and Oceanography* 10 (Supplement): 97-102.

Englehardt, D. W.
365   1960 A Comparative Study of Two Early Wisconsin Bogs in Indiana. *Indiana Academy of Science Proceedings* 69: 110-118.

366   1965 A Late-Glacial - Post-Glacial Pollen Chronology for Indiana. *American Journal of Science* 263: 410-415.

Evans, G. L.
367   1951 Prehistoric Wells in Eastern New Mexico. *American Antiquity* 17: 1-9.

Evans, G. L., and G. E. Meade
368   1945 Quaternary of the Texas High Plains. *University of Texas Publications* 4401: 485-507.

Fagan, J. L.
369   1974 Altithermal Occupation of Spring Sites in the Northern Great Basin. *University of Oregon Anthropological Papers* 6.

Falconer, G.
370   1966 Preservation of Vegetation and Patterned Ground under a Thin Ice Body in Northern Baffin Island, N. W. T. *Geographical Bulletin* 8: 194-200.

Farnham, R. S., J. H. McAndrews, and H. E. Wright, Jr.
371   1964 A Late-Wisconsin Buried Soil near Aitkin, Minnesota and its Paleobotanical Setting. *American Journal of Science* 262: 393-412.

Farrand, W. R., R. Zahner, and W. S. Benninghoff
372   1969 Cary-Port Huron Interstade: Evidence from a Buried Bryophyte Bed, Cheboygan County, Michigan. Geological Society of America Special Paper 123: 249-262.

Ferguson, C. W., Jr.
373   1968 Bristlecone Pine: Science and Aesthetics. Science 159: 839-846.

Ferguson, C. W., Jr., and D. M. Black
374   1952 Tree-Ring Chronologies on the North Rim of the Grand Canyon. Tree-Ring Bulletin 19: 12-18.

Fernald, M. L.
375   1935 Critical Plants of the Upper Great Lakes Region of Ontario and Michigan. Rhodora 37: 197-222.

Feth, J. H.
376   1959 Re-Evaluation of the Salt Chronology of Several Great Basin Lakes: A Discussion. Geological Society of America Bulletin 70: 637-640.

Field, W. O., Jr., and C. J. Heusser
377   1954 Glacier and Botanical Studies in the Canadian Rockies, 1953. Canadian Alpine Journal 37: 128-140.

Findley, J. S., and C. J. Jones
378   1962 Distribution and Variation of Voles of the Genus Microtus in New Mexico and Adjacent Areas. Journal of Mammalogy 43: 154-166.

Fisher, D. W., and J. H. Ostrom
379   1952 A Contribution to the Pleistocene Fauna of New York State. <u>American Journal of Science</u> 250: 609-616.

Fisher, R. G.
380   1935 The Relation of North American Prehistory to Post-Glacial Climatic Fluctuations. <u>University of New Mexico Bulletin, Monograph Series</u> 1(2).

Fitting, J. E.
381   1968 Environmental Potential and the Postglacial Readaptation in Eastern North America. <u>American Antiquity</u> 33: 441-445.

Fitting, J. E., J. de Visscher, and E. S. Wahla
382   1966 The Paleo-Indian Occupation of the Holcombe Beach. <u>Museum of Anthropology, University of Michigan, Anthropological Papers</u> 27.

Fitzhugh, W. W.
383   1972 Environmental Archaeology and Cultural Systems in Hamilton Inlet, Laborador. <u>Smithsonian Contributions to Anthropology</u> 16.

Flerow, C. C.
384   1967 On the Origin of the Mammalian Fauna of Canada. In, D. M. Hopkins (ed.), <u>The Bering Land Bridge</u>, pp. 271-280. Stanford University Press, Palo Alto.

Flint, R. F.
385   1947 <u>Glacial Geology and the Pleistocene Epoch</u>. John Wiley and Sons, New York.

386   1956 New Radiocarbon Dates and Late-Pleistocene Stratigraphy. American Journal of Science 254: 265-287.

387   1957 Glacial and Pleistocene Geology. John Wiley and Sons, New York.

388   1971 Glacial and Quaternary Geology. John Wiley and Sons, New York.

Flint, R. F., and F. Brandtner
389   1961 Climatic Changes since the Last Interglacial. American Journal of Science 259: 321-328.

390   1961 Outline of Climatic Fluctuations since the Last Interglacial Age. New York Academy of Sciences Annals 95: 457-460.

Flint, R. F., and E. S. Deevey, Jr.
391   1951 Radiocarbon Dating of Late-Pleistocene Events. American Journal of Science 249: 257-300.

Flint, R. F., and W. A. Gale
392   1958 Stratigraphy and Radiocarbon Dates at Searles Lake, California. American Journal of Science 256: 689-714.

Florin, M. -B.
393   1970 Late-Glacial Diatoms of Kirchner Marsh, Southeastern Minnesota. Beihefte Zur Nova Hedwigia 31: 667-756.

Florin, M. -B., and H. E. Wright, Jr.
394   1969 Diatom Evidence for the Persistence of Stagnant Glacial Ice in Minnesota. Geological Society of America Bulletin 80: 695-704.

Follett, W. I.
395   1967 Fish Remains from Coprolites and Midden Deposits at Lovelock Cave, Churchill County, Nevada. <u>University of California Archaeological Survey Reports</u> 70: 93-116.

Forbis, R. G.
396   1968 Alberta. In, W. W. Caldwell (ed.), The Northwestern Plains: A Symposium. <u>The Center for Indian Studies, Occasional Paper</u> 1: 37-44. Rocky Mountain College, Billings.

397   1968 Fletcher: A Paleo-Indian Site in Alberta. <u>American Antiquity</u> 33: 1-10.

Fowler, D. D.
398   1972 Editor's Introduction. In, D. D. Fowler (ed.), Great Basin Cultural Ecology: A Symposium. <u>Desert Research Institute Publications in the Social Sciences</u> 8: 1-3. University of Nevada, Reno.

Fowler, D. D. (ed.)
399   1972 Great Basin Cultural Ecology: A Symposium. <u>Desert Research Institute Publications in the Social Sciences</u> 8. University of Nevada, Reno.

Fowler, D. D., D. B. Madsen, and E. M. Hattori
400   1972 Archaeology of Southeast Nevada. <u>Desert Research Institute Publications in the Social Sciences</u> 6. University of Nevada, Reno.

Frankforter, W. D.
401   1967 Faunal Study of Large Ruminants from Mill Creek Culture Sites in Northeast Iowa. In D. A. Baerreis and R. A. Bryson (eds.), Climatic Change and the Mill Creek Culture of Iowa. Archives of Archaeology 29: 511-546. Society for American Archaeology.

Freeman, C. E.
402   1972 Pollen Study of some Holocene Alluvial Deposits in Dona Ana County, Southern New Mexico. Texas Journal of Science 24: 203-220.

Frenzel, B.
403   1966 Climatic Change in the Atlantic/Sub-Boreal Transition on the Northern Hemisphere: Botanical Evidence. In, J. S. Sawyer (ed.), Proceedings of the International Symposium on World Climate 8000 to 0 B. C., pp. 99-123. Royal Meteorological Society, London.

Frey, D. G.
404   1951 Pollen Succession in the Sediments of Singletary Lake, North Carolina. Ecology 32: 518-533.

405   1953 Regional Aspects of the Late-Glacial and Post-Glacial Pollen Succession of Southeastern North Carolina. Ecological Monographs 23: 289-313.

406   1955 A Time Revision of the Pleistocene Pollen Chronology of Southeastern North Carolina. Ecology 36: 762-763.

407   1955 Stages in the Ontogeny of the Carolina Bays. International Association of Theoretical and Applied Limnology Proceedings 12: 660-668.

408 1959 The Two Creeks Interval in Indiana Pollen Diagrams. <u>Investigations of Indiana Lakes and Streams</u> 5: 131-139.

Fries, M.
409 1962 Pollen Profiles of Late Pleistocene and Recent Sediments from Weber Lake, Minnesota. <u>Ecology</u> 43: 295-308.

Fries, M., H. E. Wright, Jr., and M. Rubin
410 1961 A Late Wisconsin Buried Peat at North Branch, Minnesota. <u>American Journal of Science</u> 259: 679-693.

Friesner, R. C., and J. E. Potzger
411 1946 The Cabin Creek Raised Bog, Randolph County, Indiana. <u>Butler University Botanical Studies</u> 8: 24-41.

Fritts, H. C.
412 1965 Dendrochronology. In, H. E. Wright, Jr., and D. G. Frey (eds.), <u>The Quaternary of the United States</u>, pp. 871-879. Princeton University Press, Princeton.

413 1965 Tree-Ring Evidence for Climatic Changes in Western North America. <u>Monthly Weather Review</u> 93: 421-443.

Fritts, H. C., D. G. Smith, and M. A. Stokes
414 1965 The Biological Model for Palaeoclimatic Interpretation of Mesa Verde Tree-Ring Series. <u>Society for American Archaeology Memoir</u> 19: 101-121.

Fritts, H. C., et. al.
415   1971 Multivariate Techniques for Specifying Tree-Growth and Climate Relationships and for Reconstructing Anomalies in Paleoclimate. Journal of Applied Meteorology 10: 845-864.

Frye, J. C., and A. B. Leonard
416   1957 Ecological Interpretations of Pliocene and Pleistocene Stratigraphy in the Great Plains Region. American Journal of Science 255: 1-11.

Fryxell, R.
417   1964 Regional Patterns of Sedimentation Recorded by Cave and Rockshelter Stratigraphy in the Columbia Plateau, Washington. Geological Society of America Special Paper 76: 273.

418   1964 Summary of Postglacial History of the Columbia Plateau, Washington. Washington State University Laboratory of Anthropology, Report of Investigations 27: 30-31.

Fryxell, R., and R. D. Daugherty
419   1963 Late Glacial and Postglacial Geological and Archaeological Chronology of the Columbia Plateau, Washington. Washington State University Laboratory of Anthropology, Report of Investigations 23.

Fuller, G.
420   1929 Peat Bogs and Postglacial Vegetation. Botanical Gazette 87: 560-562.

421   1935 Post-Glacial Vegetation of the Lake Michigan Region. Ecology 16: 473-487.

422   1939 Interglacial and Post-Glacial Vegetation of Illinois. Illinois Academy of Science Transactions 32: 5-15.

Funk, R. E.
423   1972 Early Man in the Northeast and the Late-Glacial Environment. Man in the Northeast 4: 7-39.

Funk, R. E., D. W. Fisher, and E. M. Reilly, Jr.
424   1970 Caribou and Paleo-Indian in New York State: A Presumed Association. American Journal of Science 268: 181-186.

Funk, R. E., G. F. Walters, and W. F. Ehlers
425   1969 A Radiocarbon Date for Early Man from the Dutchess Quarry Cave. New York State Archeological Association Bulletin 46: 19-21.

Gale, H. S.
426   1915 Geologic History of Lake Lahontan. Science 41: 209-211.

427   1915 Salines in the Owens, Searles, and Panamint Basins, Southeastern California. United States Geological Survey Bulletin 580: 251-323.

Galinat, W. C.
428   1959 Plant Remains from the LoDaiska Site. Denver Museum of Natural History Proceedings 8: 104-113.

Gallein, L., and J. G. Ogden III
429   1965 Pollen Diagrams of Torren's Bog, Licking County, Ohio. International Association for Quaternary Research, Seventh Congress, Guidebook G: 80.

Garrison, G. C.
430 1967 Pollen Stratigraphy and Age of an Early Postglacial Beaver Site near Columbus, Ohio. Ohio Journal of Science 67: 96-105.

Gehlbach, F. R., and R. R. Miller
431 1961 Fishes from Archaeological Sites in Northern New Mexico. Southwestern Naturalist 6: 2-8.

Gehris, C. W.
432 1965 Pollen Analysis of the Cranberry Bog Preserve, Tannersville, Monroe County, Pennsylvania. Dissertation Abstracts 25: 4327.

Geis, J. W., and W. R. Boggess
433 1968 The Prairie Peninsula: Its Origin and Significance in the Vegetational History of Central Illinois. In, R. E. Bergstrom (ed.), The Quaternary of Illinois. University of Illinois College of Agriculture Special Publication 14: 89-95.

Giddings, J. L., Jr.
434 1941 Dendrochronology in Northern Alaska. Bulletin of the University of Arizona 12(4); Laboratory of Tree-Ring Research Bulletin 1; University of Alaska Publications 4.

435 1947 Mackenzie River Delta Chronology. Tree-Ring Bulletin 13: 26-29.

436 1948 Chronology of the Kobuk-Kotzebue Sites. Tree-Ring Bulletin 14: 26-32.

Gilliam, J. A., R. O. Kapp, and R. D. Bogue
437   1967 A Post-Wisconsin Pollen Sequence from Vestaburg Bog, Montcalm County, Michigan. Papers of the Michigan Academy of Science, Arts and Letters 52: 3-17.

Gladwin, H. S.
438   n. d. Tree-Ring Analysis, Tree-Rings, and Droughts. Medallion Papers 37. Gila Pueblo, Globe, Arizona.

Gleason, H. A.
439   1909 Some Unsolved Problems of the Prairies. Bulletin of the Torrey Botanical Club 36: 265-271.

440   1922 The Vegetational History of the Middle West. Annals of the Association of American Geographers 12: 39-85.

Glock, W. S.
441   1955 Growth Rings and Climate. Botanical Review 21: 73-188.

Goggin, J. M.
442   1948 Florida Archaeology and Recent Ecological Changes. Washington Academy of Sciences Journal 38: 225-233.

Goldthwait, R. P.
443   1958 Wisconsin Age Forests in Western Ohio. I. Age and Glacial Events. Ohio Journal of Science 58: 209-219.

444   1963 Dating the Little Ice Age in Glacier Bay, Alaska. Twenty First International Geological Congress Report, Part 27: 37-46.

445 1966 Evidence from Alaskan Glaciers of Major Climatic Changes. In, J. S. Sawyer (ed.), <u>Proceedings of the International Symposium on World Climate 8000 to 0 B. C.</u>, pp. 40-53. Royal Meteorological Society, London.

446 1966 Glacial History. In, R. P. Goldthwait, et. al., Soil Development and Ecological Succession in a Deglaciated Area of Muir Inlet, South-east Alaska. <u>Ohio State University Research Foundation Institute of Polar Studies Report</u> 20: 1-18.

Goldthwait, R. P., I. C. McKellar, and C. Cronk
447 1963 Fluctuations of Crillon Glacier System, Southeast Alaska. <u>International Association of Scientific Hydrology Bulletin</u> 8: 62-74.

Gooding, A. M., and J. G. Ogden III
448 1965 A Radiocarbon Dated Pollen Sequence from the Wells Mastodon Site near Rochester, Indiana. <u>Ohio Journal of Science</u> 65: 1-11.

Gorman, F.
449 1972 The Clovis Hunters: An Alternative View of Their Environment and Ecology. In, M. P. Leone (ed.), <u>Contemporary Archaeology</u>, pp. 206-221. Southern Illinois University Press, Carbondale and Edwardsville.

Graham, A.
450 1964 Origin and Evolution of the Biota of Southeastern North America: Evidence from the Fossil Pollen Record. <u>Evolution</u> 18: 571-585.

Graham, A., and C. Heimsch
451 1960 Pollen Studies of some Texas Peat Deposits. <u>Ecology</u> 41: 751-763.

Grayson, J. F.

452   1954 Evidence of Four Pine Species from Fossil Pollen in Michigan. Ecology 35: 327-331.

453   1958 The Post-Glacial History of Vegetation and Climate in the Labrador-Quebec Region as Determined by Palynology. Dissertation Abstracts 18: 1229.

Green, F. E.

454   1962 Additional Notes on Prehistoric Wells at the Clovis Site. American Antiquity 28: 230-234.

Gregory, H. B.

455   1917 Geology of the Navajo Country. United States Geological Survey Professional Paper 93.

Griffin, C. D.

456   1950 A Pollen Profile from Reed Bog, Randolph County, Indiana. Butler University Botanical Studies 9: 131-139.

457   1951 Pollen Analysis of a Peat Deposit in Livingston County, Illinois. Butler University Botanical Studies 10: 90-99.

Griffin, J. B.

458   1960 A Hypothesis for the Prehistory of the Winnebago. In, S. Diamond (ed.), Culture in History, pp. 809-868. Columbia University Press, New York.

459   1960 Climatic Change: A Contributing Cause of the Growth and Decline of Northern Hopewellian Culture. Wisconsin Archeologist 41: 21-33.

460 1961 Post-Glacial Ecology and Culture Changes in the Great Lakes Area of North America. <u>University of Michigan Great Lakes Research Division Publication</u> 7: 147-155.

461 1961 Some Correlations of Climatic and Cultural Change in Eastern North American Prehistory. <u>New York Academy of Sciences Annals</u> 95: 710-717.

462 1965 Late Quaternary Prehistory in the Northeastern Woodlands. In, H. E. Wright, Jr., and D. G. Frey (eds.), <u>The Quaternary of the United States</u>, pp. 655-667. Princeton University Press, Princeton.

463 1968 Observations on Illinois Prehistory in Late Pleistocene and Early Recent Times. In, R. E. Bergstrom (ed.), The Quaternary of Illinois. <u>University of Illinois College of Agriculture Special Publication</u> 14: 123-137.

Griffin, J. W., and D. E. Wray
464 1945 Bison in Illinois Archaeology. <u>Illinois Academy of Science Transactions</u> 38: 21-26.

Griggs, G. B., et. al.
465 1970 Holocene Faunal Stratigraphy and Paleoclimatic Implications of Deep-Sea Sediments in Cascadia Basin. <u>Palaeogeography, Palaeoclimatology, Palaeoecology</u> 7: 5-12.

Griggs, R. F.
466 1934 The Edge of the Forest in Alaska and the Reasons for its Position. <u>Ecology</u> 15: 80-96.

467 1937 Timberlines as Indicators of Climatic Trends. <u>Science</u> 85: 251-255.

Grüger, E.
468 1970 The Development of the Vegetation of Southern Illinois since Late Illinoian Time (Preliminary Report). Revue de Géographie Physique et de Géologie Dynamique (2), 12, Fascicule 2: 143-148.

469 1972 Pollen and Seed Studies of Wisconsinan Vegetation in Illinois, U. S. A. Geological Society of America Bulletin 83: 2715-2734.

Grüger, J.
470 1972 Late Quaternary Vegetation Development in South-Central Illinois. Quaternary Research 2: 217-231.

471 1973 Studies on the Late Quaternary Vegetation of Northeastern Kansas. Geological Society of America Bulletin 84: 239-250.

Gruhn, R.
472 1961 The Archaeology of Wilson Butte Cave. Occasional Papers of the Idaho State College Museum 6.

Guennel, G. K.
473 1950 History of Forests in the Glacial Lake Chicago Area. Butler University Botanical Studies 9: 149-158.

Guilday, J. E.
474 1961 Prehistoric Record of Scalopus from Western Pennsylvania. Journal of Mammalogy 42: 117-118.

475 1962 The Pleistocene Local Fauna of the Natural Chimneys, Augusta County, Virginia. Carnegie Museum Annals 36: 87-122.

476   1967 Differential Extinction during Late-Pleistocene and Recent Times. In, P. S. Martin and H. E. Wright (eds.), Pleistocene Extinctions, pp. 121-140. Yale University Press. New Haven.

477   1967 The Climatic Significance of the Hosterman's Pit Local Fauna, Centre County, Pennsylvania. American Antiquity 32: 231-232.

478   1968 Archaeological Evidence of Caribou from New York and Massachusetts. Journal of Mammalogy 49: 344-345.

479   1968 Grizzly Bears from Eastern North America. American Midland Naturalist 79: 247-250.

480   1969 A Possible Caribou - Paleo-Indian Association from Dutchess Quarry Cave, Orange County. New York. New York State Archeological Association Bulletin 45: 24-29.

481   1969 Bone Refuse from the Lamoka Lake Site. In, W. A. Ritchie, The Archaeology of New York State, pp. 54-59. Second Edition. Natural History Press, New York.

482   1969 Small Mammal Remains from the Wasden Site (Owl Cave), Bonneville County, Idaho. Tebiwa 12(1): 47-57.

483   1971 The Pleistocene History of the Appalachian Mammal Fauna. In, P. C. Holt (ed.), The Distributional History of the Biota of the Southern Appalachians. Part III: Vertebrates. Virginia Polytechnic Institute and State University Research Division Monograph 4: 233-262.

Guilday, J. E., and E. K. Adam
484   1967 Small Mammal Remains from Jaguar Cave, Lemhi County, Idaho. Tebiwa 10(1): 26-36.

Guilday, J. E., and M. E. Bender
485   1960 Late Pleistocene Records of the Yellow-cheeked Vole, Microtus xanthognathus (Leach). Carnegie Museum Annals 35: 315-330.

Guilday, J. E., and P. W. Parmalee
486   1965 Animal Remains from the Sheep Rock Shelter, Huntingdon County, Pennsylvania. Pennsylvania Archaeologist 35: 34-49.

487   1972 Quaternary Periglacial Records of Voles of the Genus Phenacomys Merriam (Cricetidae: Rodentia). Quaternary Research 2: 170-175.

Guilday, J. E., H. W. Hamilton, and A. D. McCrady
488   1966 The Bone Breccia of Bootlegger Sink, York County, Pa. Carnegie Museum Annals 38: 145-163.

489   1971 The Welsh Cave Peccaries (Platygonus) and Associated Fauna, Kentucky Pleistocene. Carnegie Museum Annals 43: 249-320.

Guilday, J. E., P. S. Martin, and A. D. McCrady
490   1964 New Paris No. 4: A Pleistocene Cave Deposit in Bedford County, Pennsylvania. National Speleological Society Bulletin 26: 121-194.

Guthrie, R. D.
491   1968 Paleoecology of a Late Pleistocene Small Mammal Community from Interior Alaska. Arctic 21: 223-244.

492   1968 Paleoecology of the Large Mammal Community in Interior Alaska during the Late Pleistocene. American Midland Naturalist 79: 346-363.

Hack, J. T.

493   1939 The Late Quaternary History of Several Valleys of Northern Arizona. Northern Arizona Museum Notes II: 67-73.

494   1941 Dunes of the Western Navajo Country. Geographical Review 31: 240-263.

495   1942 The Changing Environment of the Hopi Indians of Arizona. Peabody Museum of Archaeology and Ethnology Papers 34(1).

496   1943 Antiquity of the Finley Site. American Antiquity 8: 235-241.

497   1945 Recent Geology of the Tsegi Canyon. In, R. L. Beals, G. W. Brainerd, and W. Smith, A Report on the Archaeological Work of the Rainbow Bridge - Monument Valley Expedition. University of California Publications in American Archaeology and Ethnology 44(1): 151-158.

498   1969 The Area, Its Geology: Cenozoic Development of the Southern Appalachians. In, P. C. Holt (ed.), The Distributional History of the Biota of the Southern Appalachians. Part I: Invertebrates. Virginia Polytechnic Institute Research Division Monographs 1: 1-18.

Hafsten, U.
499   1961 Pleistocene Development of Vegetation and Climate in the Southern High Plains as Evidenced by Pollen Analysis. In, F. Wendorf (ed.), Paleoecology of the Llano Estacado. Fort Burgwin Research Center Publications I: 59-91. Museum of New Mexico Press, Sante Fe.

500   1964 A Standard Pollen Diagram for the Southern High Plains, U. S. A., Covering the Period Back to the Early Wisconsin Glaciation. International Association for Quaternary Research, Sixth Congress Report 2: 407-420.

501   1970 A Sub-Division of the Late Pleistocene Period on a Synchronous Basis, Intended for Global and Universal Usage. Palaeogeography, Palaeoclimatology, Palaeoecology 7: 279-296.

Hamp, F.
502   1940 A Fossil Pollen Study of Two Northern Indiana Bogs. Butler University Pollen Studies 4: 217-225.

Handley, C. O., Jr.
503   1971 Appalachian Mammalian Geography - Recent Epoch. In, P. C. Holt (ed.), The Distributional History of the Biota of the Southern Appalachians. Part III: Vertebrates. Virginia Polytechnic Institute and State University Research Division Monographs 4: 263-303.

Hansen, G. H.
504   1934 An Interpretation of Past Climatic Cycles from Observations Made of Utah Lake Sediments. Utah Academy of Sciences, Arts, and Letters Proceedings II: 161-162.

Hansen, H. P.

505 1937 Pollen Analysis of Two Wisconsin Bogs of Different Ages. Ecology 18: 136-148.

506 1938 Postglacial Forest Succession and Climate in the Puget Sound Region. Ecology 19: 528-542.

507 1939 Paleoecology of a Central Washington Bog. Ecology 20: 563-568.

508 1939 Pollen Analysis of a Bog in Northern Idaho. American Journal of Botany 26: 225-228.

509 1939 Pollen Analysis of a Bog near Spokane, Washington. Bulletin of the Torrey Botanical Club 66: 215-220.

510 1939 Postglacial Vegetation of the Driftless Area in Wisconsin. American Midland Naturalist 21: 752-762.

511 1940 Paleoecology of a Montane Peat Deposit at Bonaparte Lake, Washington. Northwest Science 14: 60-69.

512 1940 Paleoecology of Two Peat Bogs in Southwestern British Columbia. American Journal of Botany 27: 144-149.

513 1941 A Pollen Study of Post-Pleistocene Lake Sediments in the Upper Sonoran Life Zone of Washington. American Journal of Science 239: 503-522.

514 1941 Further Pollen Studies of Post-Pleistocene Bogs in the Puget Lowland of Washington. Bulletin of the Torrey Botanical Club 68: 133-148.

515 1941 Paleoecology of a Bog in the Spruce-Hemlock Climax of the Olympic Peninsula. American Midland Naturalist 25: 290-297.

516 1941 Paleoecology of a Montane Peat Deposit near Lake Wenatchee, Washington. Northwest Science 15: 53-65.

517 1941 Paleoecology of a Peat Deposit in West Central Oregon. American Journal of Botany 28: 206-212.

518 1941 Paleoecology of Two Peat Deposits on the Oregon Coast. Oregon State Monographs, Studies in Botany 3: 1-31. Oregon State University, Corvallis.

519 1942 A Pollen Study of a Montane Peat Deposit near Mount Adams, Washington. Lloydia 5: 305-313.

520 1942 A Pollen Study of Lake Sediments in the Lower Willamette Valley of Western Oregon. Bulletin of the Torrey Botanical Club 69: 262-280.

521 1942 A Pollen Study of Peat Profiles from Lower Klamath Lake of Oregon and California. In, L. S. Cressman, Archaeological Researches in the Northern Great Basin. Carnegie Institute of Washington Publication 538: 103-114.

522 1942 Post-Mount Mazama Forest Succession on the East Slope of the Central Cascades of Oregon. American Midland Naturalist 27: 523-534.

523 1942 The Influence of Volcano Eruptions upon Post-Pleistocene Forest Succession in Central Oregon. American Journal of Botany 29: 214-219.

524   1943 A Pollen Study of a Subalpine Bog in the Blue Mountains of Northeastern Oregon. Ecology 24: 40-78.

525   1943 A Pollen Study of Two Bogs on Orcas Island, of the San Juan Islands, Washington. Bulletin of the Torrey Botanical Club 70: 236-243.

526   1943 Paleoecology of a Peat Deposit in East Central Washington. Northwest Science 17: 35-40.

527   1943 Paleoecology of Two Sand Dune Bogs on the Southern Oregon Coast. American Journal of Botany 30: 335-340.

528   1943 Post-Pleistocene Forest Succession in Northern Idaho. American Midland Naturalist 30: 796-802.

529   1944 Further Pollen Studies of Peat Bogs on the Pacific Boast of Oregon and Washington. Bulletin of the Torrey Botanical Club 71: 627-636.

530   1944 Postglacial Vegetation of Eastern Washington. Northwest Science 18: 79-87.

531   1946 Early Man in Oregon. Pollen Analysis and Postglacial Climate and Chronology. Scientific Monthly 62: 52-62.

532   1946 Postglacial Forest Succession and Climate in the Oregon Cascades. American Journal of Science 244: 710-734.

533 1947 Climate Versus Fire and Soil as Factors in Post-Glacial Forest Succession in the Puget Lowland of Washington. American Journal of Science 245: 265-286.

534 1947 Postglacial Forest Succession, Climate, and Chronology in the Pacific Northwest. American Philosophical Society Transactions 37.

535 1947 Postglacial Vegetation of the Northern Great Basin. American Journal of Botany 34: 164-171.

536 1948 Postglacial Forests of the Glacier National Park Region. Ecology 29: 146-152.

537 1949 Postglacial Forests in South Central Alberta, Canada. American Journal of Botany 36: 54-65.

538 1949 Postglacial Forests in West Central Alberta, Canada. Bulletin of the Torrey Botanical Club 76: 278-289.

539 1950 Pollen Analysis of Three Bogs on Vancouver Island, Canada. Journal of Ecology 38: 270-276.

540 1950 Postglacial Forests along the Alaska Highway, British Columbia. American Philosophical Society Proceedings 94: 411-421.

541 1951 Pollen Analysis of Peat Sections from near the Finley Site, Wyoming. In, J. H. Moss (ed.), et. al., Early Man in the Eden Valley, Wyoming, pp. 111-118. University of Pennsylvania Monographs.

542 1952 Postglacial Forests in the Grande Prairie - Lesser Slave Lake Region of Alberta, Canada. Ecology 33: 31-41.

543   1953 Postglacial Forests in the Yukon Territory and Alaska. American Journal of Science 251: 505-542.

544   1955 Postglacial Forests in South Central and Central British Columbia. American Journal of Science 253: 640-658.

545   1961 Cycles and Geochronology. California Academy of Sciences Occasional Papers 31.

546   1967 Chronology of Postglacial Pollen Profiles in the Pacific Northwest (U. S. A.). Review of Palaeobotany and Palynology 4: 103-105.

Hansen, H. P., and I. S. Allison
547   1942 A Pollen Study of a Fossil Peat Deposit on the Oregon Coast. Northwest Science 16: 86-92.

Hansen, H. P., and E. L. Packard
548   1949 Pollen Analysis and the Age of the Proboscidean Bones near Silverton, Oregon. Ecology 30: 461-469.

Hanson, G.
549   1934 The Bear River Delta and its Significance Regarding Pleistocene and Recent Glaciation. Royal Society of Canada Transactions, Section 4, Series 3 28: 179-185.

Harding, S. T.
550   1935 Changes in Lake Levels in the Great Basin Area. Civil Engineering 5: 87-92.

551   1942 Lakes. In, O. E. Meinzer (ed.), Hydrology, pp. 220-243. McGraw-Hill, New York.

Hare, F. K.

552   1952 Post-Glacial Climatic Changes in Eastern Canada. Canadian Branch, Royal Meteorological Society, Papers 2(7): 8-18.

553   1973 On the Climatology of Post-Wisconsin Events in Canada. Arctic and Alpine Research 5: 169-170.

Hargrave, L. L.

554   1939 Bird Bones from Abandoned Indian Dwellings in Arizona and Utah. Condor 41: 206-210.

Harper, K. T., and G. M. Alder

555   1970 The Macroscopic Plant Remains of the Deposits of Hogup Cave, Utah, and the Paleoclimatic Interpretation. In, C. M. Aikens, Hogup Cave. University of Utah Anthropological Papers 93: 215-240.

556   1972 Paleoclimatic Inferences Concerning the Last 10,000 Years from a Resampling of Danger Cave, Utah. In, D. D. Fowler (ed.), Great Basin Cultural Ecology: A Symposium. Desert Research Institute Publications in the Social Sciences 8: 13-23. University of Nevada, Reno.

Harris, A. H.

557   1963 Vertebrate Remains and Past Environmental Reconstruction in the Navajo Reservoir District. Museum of New Mexico Papers in Anthropology 11.

558   1970 Past Climates of the Navajo Reservoir District. American Antiquity 35: 374-377.

Harris, A. H., and J. S. Findley
559   1964 Pleistocene - Recent Fauna of the Isleta Caves, Bernalillo County, New Mexico. American Journal of Science 262: 114-120.

Harrison, A. E.
560   1956 Fluctuations of the Nisqually Glacier, Mt. Rainier, Washington, since 1750. Journal of Glaciology 2: 675-683.

561   1956 Multiple Glaciation since the Ice Ages. Science 124: 181-182.

Harrison, W., et. al.
562   1965 Possible Late-Pleistocene Uplift, Chesapeake Bay Entrance. Journal of Geology 73: 201-229.

Haselton, G. M.
563   1966 Glacial Geology of Muir Inlet, Southeast Alaska. Ohio State University Research Foundation Institute of Polar Studies Report 18.

Hattersley-Smith, G.
564   1969 Glacial Features of Tanqueray Fiord and Adjoining Areas of Northern Ellesmere Island, N. W. T. Journal of Glaciology 8: 23-50.

565   1972 Climatic Change and Related Problems in Northern Ellesmere Island, N. W. T., Canada. In, Y. Vasari, H. Hyvärinen, and S. Hicks (eds.), Climatic Changes in Arctic Areas during the Last Ten-Thousand Years. Acta Universitatis Ouluensis, Series A: Scientiae Rerum Naturalium 3, Geologica 1: 137-148. University of Oulu, Oulu.

Haury, E. W.
566   1934 Climate and Human History. <u>Tree-Ring Bulletin</u> 1: 13-15.

567   1950 Final Discussion. In, E. W. Haury, et. al., The <u>Stratigraphy and Archaeology of Ventana Cave</u>, pp. 521-548. The University of New Mexico and the University of Arizona Presses, Albuquerque and Tucson.

568   1958 Post-Pleistocene Human Occupation of the Southwest. In, T. L. Smiley (ed.), Climate and Man in the Southwest. <u>University of Arizona Bulletin</u> 28(4): 69-75.

Haury, E. W., E. B. Sayles, and W. W. Wasley
569   1959 The Lehner Mammoth Site, Southeastern Arizona. <u>American Antiquity</u> 25: 2-30.

Hawley, F.
570   1939 New Applications of Tree Ring Analysis. In, D. D. Brand and F. E. Harvey (eds.), <u>So Live the Works of Men</u>, pp. 177-186. University of New Mexico Press, Albuquerque.

571   1941 Tree-Ring Analysis and Dating in the Mississippi Drainage. <u>University of Chicago Publications in Anthropology, Occasional Papers</u> 2.

Haynes, C. V., Jr.
572   1966 Geochronology of Late Quaternary Alluvium. <u>Geochronology Laboratories, University of Arizona, Interim Research Report</u> 10.

573 1967 Quaternary Geology of the Tule Springs Area, Clark County, Nevada. In, H. M. Wormington and D. Ellis (eds.), Pleistocene Studies in Southern Nevada. <u>Nevada State Museum Anthropological Papers</u> 13: 15-104.

574 1968 Geochronology of Late Quaternary Alluvium. In, R. B. Morrison and H. E. Wright, Jr. (eds.), <u>Means of Correlation of Quaternary Successions</u>, pp. 591-631. University of Utah Press, Salt Lake City.

575 1973 Geochronology and Paleo-Hydrology of the Murray Springs Clovis Site, Arizona. <u>Abstracts with Programs</u> 5(7): 659. Geological Society of America.

Haynes, C. V., Jr., and G. Agogino
576 1960 Geological Significance of a New Radiocarbon Date from the Lindenmeier Site. <u>Denver Museum of Natural History Proceedings</u> 9.

577 1965 Prehistoric Springs and Geochronology of the Clovis Site, New Mexico. <u>American Antiquity</u> 31: 812-821.

Haynes, C. V., Jr., and D. L. Grey
578 1965 The Sister's Hill Site and its Bearing upon the Wyoming Postglacial Alluvial Chronology. <u>Plains Anthropologist</u> 10: 196-207.

Hegg, O.
579 1963 Palynological Studies of a Peat Deposit in Front of the Thompson Glacier. <u>Axel Heiberg Island Research Reports, McGill University, Preliminary Report</u>, 1961-1962: 217-219.

Heizer, R. F.
580   1951 Preliminary Report on the Leonard Rockshelter Site, Pershing County, Nevada. American Antiquity 17: 89-98.

Heizer, R. F., and L. K. Napton
581   1970 Archaeological Investigations in Lovelock Cave, Nevada. In, R. F. Heizer, et. al., Archaeology and the Prehistoric Great Basin Lacustrine Subsistence Pattern as Seen from Lovelock Cave, Nevada. Contributions of the University of California Archaeological Research Facility 10: 1-86.

Henning, D. R., A. E. Henning, and D. A. Baerreis
582   1967 1963 Excavations in the Mill Creek Sites. In, D. A. Baerreis and R. A. Bryson (eds.), Climatic Change and the Mill Creek Culture of Iowa. Archives of Archaeology 29: 62-187. Society for American Archaeology.

Hester, J. J.
583   1967 The Agency of Man in Animal Extinctions. In, P. S. Martin and H. E. Wright, Jr. (eds.), Pleistocene Extinctions, pp. 169-192. Yale University Press, New Haven.

Hester, T. R.
584   1973 Chronological Ordering of Great Basin Prehistory. Contributions of the University of California Archaeological Research Facility 17.

Heusser, C. J.
585   1952 Pollen Profiles from Southeastern Alaska. Ecological Monographs 22: 331-352.

586 1953 Radiocarbon Dating of the Thermal Maximum in Southeastern Alaska. Ecology 34: 637-640.

587 1954 Additional Pollen Profiles from Southeastern Alaska. American Journal of Science 252: 106-119.

588 1954 Alpine Fir at Taku Glacier, Alaska, with Notes on its Postglacial Migration to the Territory. Bulletin of the Torrey Botanical Club 81: 83-86.

589 1955 Pollen Profiles from Prince William Sound and Southeastern Kenai Peninsula, Alaska. Ecology 36: 185-202.

590 1955 Pollen Profiles from the Queen Charlotte Islands, British Columbia. Canadian Journal of Botany 33: 429-449.

591 1956 Postglacial Environments in the Canadian Rockies. Ecological Monographs 26: 263-302.

592 1957 Variations of Blue, Hoh, and White Glaciers during Recent Centuries. Arctic 10: 139-150.

593 1958 Late Pleistocene Environments and Chronology of Pacific Coastal Alaska. Geological Society of America Bulletin 69: 1753-1754.

594 1959 Radiocarbon Dates of Peats from North Pacific North America. American Journal of Science Radiocarbon Supplement 1: 29-34.

595 1960 Late Pleistocene Environments of North Pacific North America. American Geographical Society Special Publications 35.

596	1961 Some Comparisons between Climatic Changes in Northwestern North America and Patagonia. <u>New York Academy of Sciences Annals</u> 95: 642-657.
597	1962 Pleistocene Palynology in Western Washington. <u>Pollen et Spores</u> 4: 350.
598	1963 Pollen Diagrams from Ogotoruk Creek, Cape Thompson, Alaska. <u>Grana Palynologica</u> 4: 149-159.
599	1963 Pollen Diagrams from Three Former Cedar Bogs in the Hackensack Tidal Marsh, Northeastern New Jersey. <u>Bulletin of the Torrey Botanical Club</u> 90: 16-28.
600	1963 Postglacial Palynology and Archaeology in the Naknek River Drainage Area, Alaska. <u>American Antiquity</u> 29: 74-81.
601	1964 Palynology of Four Bog Sections from the Western Olympic Peninsula, Washington. <u>Ecology</u> 45: 23-40.
602	1965 A Pleistocene Phytogeographical Sketch of the Pacific Northwest and Alaska. In, H. E. Wright, Jr., and D. G. Frey (eds.), <u>The Quaternary of the United States</u>, pp. 469-483. Princeton University Press, Princeton.
603	1966 Palynology of the Ogotoruk Creek Area. In, N. J. Wilimovsky and J. N. Wolfe (eds.), Environment of the Cape Thompson Region, Alaska. <u>United States Atomic Energy Commission</u> PNE-481: 355-362.

604   1966 Pleistocene Climatic Variations in the Western
           United States. In, D. I. Blumenstock (ed.),
           Pleistocene and Post-Pleistocene Climatic
           Variations in the Pacific Area, pp. 9-36. Bernice
           P. Bishop Museum, Honolulu.

605   1966 Polar Hemispheric Correlation: Palynological
           Evidence from Chile and the Pacific North-West
           of America. In, J. S. Sawyer (ed.), Proceedings
           of the International Symposium on World Climate
           8000 to 0 B. C., pp. 124-141. Royal Meteorological
           Society, London.

606   1967 Pleistocene and Postglacial Vegetation of Alaska
           and the Yukon Territory. In, H. P. Hansen (ed.),
           Arctic Biology, pp. 131-151. Oregon State University,
           Corvallis.

607   1969 Pleistocene Environments and Chronology of
           the Western Olympic Peninsula, Washington.
           Abstracts with Programs for 1969, Part 7: 99.

608   1973 Environmental Sequence Following the Fraser
           Advance of the San Juan de Fuca Lobe, Washington.
           Quaternary Research 3: 284-306.

           Heusser, C. J., and L. E. Florer
609   1973 Correlations of Marine and Continental Quaternary
           Pollen Records from the Northeast Pacific and
           Western Washington. Quaternary Research 3: 661-670.

           Heusser, C. J., and M. G. Marcus
610   1964 Historical Variations of Lemon Creek Glacier,
           Alaska, and Their Relationship to the Climatic
           Record. Journal of Glaciology 5: 77-86.

Heusser, C. J., R. L. Schuster, and A. K. Gilkey
611 1954 Geobotanical Studies on the Taku Glacier Anomaly. Geographical Review 44: 244-239.

Hevly, R. H.
612 1962 Pollen Analysis of Laguna Salada. In, Guidebook of the Mogollon Rim Region, East-Central Arizona. New Mexico Geological Society Thirteenth Field Conference, 1962: 115-117.

613 1964 Paleoecology of Laguna Salada. In, P. S. Martin, et. al. (eds.), Chapters in the Prehistory of Arizona, II. Chicago Natural History Museum, Fieldiana (Anthropology) 55: 171-187.

614 1965 Comparison of Pollen, Tree-Ring, and Cultural Records of the Colorado Plateau from 200 to 1400 A. D. International Association for Quaternary Research, Seventh Congress, General Sessions Abstracts: 213-214.

Hibbard, C. W.
615 1960 An Interpretation of Pliocene and Pleistocene Climates in North America. Michigan Academy of Science Annual Report (1959-1960) 62: 5-30.

616 1970 Pleistocene Mammalian Local Faunas from the Great Plains and Central Lowland Provinces of the United States. In, W. Dort, Jr., and J. K. Jones, Jr. (eds.), Pleistocene and Recent Environments of the Central Great Plains. Department of Geology, University of Kansas, Special Publication 3: 395-433.

Hodge, E. T.
617 1931 Stadter Buried Forest. Mazama 31: 82-86.

Hoffman, R., and J. K. Jones, Jr.
618 1970 Influence of Late-Glacial and Post-Glacial Events on the Distribution of Recent Mammals on the Northern Great Plains. In, W. Dort, Jr., and J. K. Jones, Jr. (eds.), Pleistocene and Recent Environments of the Central Great Plains. <u>Department of Geology, University of Kansas, Special Publication</u> 3: 355-394.

Holmes, G. W.
619 1951 The Regional Significance of the Pleistocene Deposits in the Eden Valley, Wyoming. In, J. H. Moss, et. al., <u>Early Man in the Eden Valley</u>, pp. 93-100. University of Pennsylvania Monographs.

Holmes, G. W., and J. H. Moss
620 1955 Pleistocene Geology of the Southwestern Wind River Mountains, Wyoming. <u>Geological Society of America Bulletin</u> 66: 629-654.

Hopkins, D. M.
621 1953 Seward Peninsula. In, T. L. Péwé, et. al., Multiple Glaciation in Alaska. <u>United States Geological Survey Circular</u> 289: 10-11.

Hopkins, D. M., and J. L. Giddings, Jr.
622 1953 Geological Background of the Iyatayet Archaeological Site, Cape Denbigh, Alaska. <u>Smithsonian Miscellaneous Collections</u> 121(11).

Hopkins, D. M., F. S. MacNeil, and E. B. Leopold
623 1961 The Coastal Plain at Nome: A Late Cenozoic Type Section for the Bering Strait Region. <u>Twenty First International Geological Congress Report</u>, Part 4: 46-57 (see "Presentation No. 51", Part 27, p. 26 for a discussion of this paper).

Horberg, L.
624   1954 Rocky Mountain and Continental Pleistocene Deposits in the Waterton Region, Alberta, Canada. Geological Society of America Bulletin 66: 1093-1150.

Horberg, L., and R. A. Robie
625   1955 Postglacial Volcanic Ash in the Rocky Mountain Piedmont, Montana and Alberta. Geological Society of America Bulletin 66: 949-956.

Horr, W. H.
626   1955 A Pollen Profile Study of the Muscotah Marsh. University of Kansas Science Bulletin 37(1): 143-149.

Hotchkiss, W. O., and L. R. Ingersoll
627   1934 Postglacial Time Calculations from Recent Geothermal Measurements. Journal of Geology 42: 113-122.

Houdek, P. K.
628   1932 Pollen Statistics for Two Indiana Bogs. Indiana Academy of Science Proceedings 42: 73-77.

629   1934 Pollen Statistics for Two Bogs in Southwestern Michigan. Papers of the Michigan Academy of Science, Arts and Letters 20: 49-56.

630   1935 Pollen Analysis of some Water Deposited Sediments. Ecology 16: 28-32.

Howard, E. B.
631   1935 The Occurrence of Flints and Extinct Animals in Pluvial Deposits near Clovis, New Mexico. Part I - Introduction. Academy of Natural Sciences of Philadelphia Proceedings 8: 299-303.

Howell, J. W.
632   1938 A Fossil Pollen Study of Kokomo Bog, Howard County, Indiana. <u>Butler University Botanical Studies</u> 4: 117-127.

Hubbard, J. P.
633   1971 The Avifauna of the Southern Appalachians: Past and Present. In, P. C. Holt (ed.), The Distributional History of the Biota of the Southern Appalachians. Part III: Vertebrates. <u>Virginia Polytechnic Institute and State University Research Division Monograph</u> 4: 197-232.

Hubbs, C. L.
634   1948 Changes in the Fish Fauna of Western North America Correlated with Changes in Ocean Temperature. <u>Journal of Marine Research</u> 7: 459-482.

635   1957 Recent Climatic History in California and Adjacent Areas. In, H. Craig (ed.), <u>Proceedings of the Conference on Recent Research in Climatology</u>, pp. 10-22. Committee on Research in Water Resources, University of California.

636   1960 Quaternary Paleoclimatology of the Pacific Coast of North America. <u>California Cooperative, Oceanic Fisheries, Investigations</u> 7: 105-112.

Hubbs, C. L., and K. F. Lagler
637   1947 Fishes of Isle Royale, Lake Superior, Michigan. <u>Papers of the Michigan Academy of Science, Arts and Letters</u> 33: 73-133.

Hubbs, C. L., and R. R. Miller
638 1948 The Zoological Evidence: Correlation between Fish Distribution and Hydrographic History in the Desert Basins of the Western United States. In, The Great Basin with Emphasis on Glacial and Postglacial Times. University of Utah Bulletin 38; Biological Series 10: 17-166.

Hubbs, C. L., and G. I. Roden
639 1964 Oceanography and Marine Life along the Pacific Coast of Middle America. In, R. C. West (ed.), Handbook of Middle American Indians, Volume I, pp. 143-186. University of Texas Press, Austin.

Hubbs, C. L., G. S. Bien, and H. E. Suess
640 1963 La Jolla Natural Radiocarbon Measurements III. Radiocarbon 5: 271.

Huffington, R. E., and C. A. Albritton
641 1941 Quaternary Sands on the Southern High Plains of Western Texas. American Journal of Science 239: 325-338.

Hunt, C. B.
642 1953 Pleistocene-Recent Boundary in the Rocky Mountain Region. United States Geological Survey Bulletin 996-A.

643 1954 Pleistocene and Recent Deposits in the Denver Area, Colorado. United States Geological Survey Bulletin 996-C.

644 1955 Recent Geology of Cone Wash, Monument Valley, Arizona. Science 122: 583-585.

Huntington, E.
645   1914 The Climatic Factor as Illustrated in Arid America. Carnegie Institute of Washington Publication 192.

646   1925 Tree Growth and Climatic Interpretations. In, Quaternary Climates. Carnegie Institute of Washington Publication 352: 155-204.

Huntington, E., and S. Visher
647   1922 Climatic Changes. Their Nature and Causes. Yale University Press, New Haven.

Hurt, W. R.
648   1953 A Comparative Study of the Preceramic Occupations of North America. American Antiquity 18: 204-222.

649   1966 The Altithermal and the Prehistory of the Northern Plains. Quaternaria 8: 101-114.

Husted, W. M.
650   1968 Wyoming. In, W. W. Caldwell (ed.), The Northwestern Plains: A Symposium. The Center for Indian Studies, Occasional Paper 1: 63-68. Rocky Mountain College, Billings.

651   1969 Bighorn Canyon Archaeology. Publications in Salvage Archaeology 12. River Basin Surveys, Smithsonian Institution, Lincoln.

652   1970 Altithermal Occupation of the Northern Rocky Mountains by Early Plains Hunting Peoples. American Quaternary Association, First Meeting, Abstracts: 69.

Hutchinson, G. E.
653 1937 A Contribution to the Limnology of Arid Regions. <u>Transactions of the Connecticut Academy of Arts and Sciences</u> 33: 47-132.

Irwin-Williams, C. J., and C. V. Haynes, Jr.
654 1970 Climatic Change and Early Population Dynamics in the Southwestern United States. <u>Quaternary Research</u> 1: 59-71.

Ives, J. D.
655 1962 Indications of Recent Extensive Glacierization in North-Central Baffin Island, N. W. T. <u>Journal of Glaciology</u> 4: 197-205.

Ives, R. L.
656 1938 Glacial Geology of the Monarch Valley, Grand County, Colorado. <u>Geological Society of America Bulletin</u> 49: 1045-1066.

657 1953 Climatic Studies in Western North America. <u>Proceedings of the Toronto Meteorological Conference, 1953</u>, pp. 218-222. Royal Meteorological Society, London.

James, W. R., and H. Nichols
658 1967 Pollen Analysis of Materials from the Phipps, Kimball, and Wittrock Sites in Iowa. In, D. A. Baerreis and R. A. Bryson (eds.), Climatic Change and the Mill Creek Culture of Iowa. <u>Archives of Archaeology</u> 29: 547-573. Society for American Archaeology.

Janson, E., and E. Halfert
659   1936 A Pollen Analysis of a Bog in Northern Ontario. Papers of the Michigan Academy of Science, Arts and Letters 22: 95-98.

Janssen, C. R.
660   1967 A Comparison between the Recent Regional Pollen Rain and the Sub-Recent Vegetation in Four Major Vegetation Types in Minnesota (U. S. A.). Review of Palaeobotany and Palynology 2: 331-342.

661   1967 Stevens Pond: A Postglacial Pollen Diagram from a Small Typha Swamp in Northwestern Minnesota Interpreted from Pollen Indicators and Surface Samples. Ecological Monographs 37: 145-172.

662   1968 Myrtle Lake: A Late and Post-Glacial Pollen Diagram from Northern Minnesota. Canadian Journal of Botany 46: 1397-1408.

Jelgersma, S.
663   1962 A Late-Glacial Pollen Diagram from Madelia, South-Central Minnesota. American Journal of Science 260: 522-529.

Jelinek, A. J.
664   1962 Review of "Paleoecology of the Llano Estacado". American Antiquity 27: 432-433.

665   1966 Correlation of Archaeological and Palynological Data. Science 152: 1507-1509.

Jenkins, D. W.
666   1950 Northward Expansion of the Maple-Basswood Forest during the Xerothermic Period. Ecological Society of America Bulletin 31: 53-54.

Jennings, J. D.
667   1957 Danger Cave. University of Utah Anthropological Papers 27.

668   1964 The Desert West. In, J. D. Jennings and F. Norbeck (eds.), Prehistoric Man in the New World, pp. 149-174. University of Chicago Press, Chicago.

669   1973 The Short, Useful Life of a Simple Hypothesis. Tebiwa 16(1): 1-9.

670   1974 Prehistory of North America. Second Edition. McGraw-Hill, New York.

Jennings, J. D. (ed.)
671   1950 Proceedings of the Sixth Plains Archaeological Conference. University of Utah Anthropological Papers 11.

Jennings, J. D., and E. Norbeck
672   1955 Great Basin Prehistory: A Review. American Antiquity 21: 1-11.

Jessup, L. T.
673   1935 Precipitation and Tree Growth in the Harney Basin, Oregon. Geographical Review 25: 310-312.

Jett, S. C.
674   1964 Pueblo Indian Migration: An Evaluation of the Possible Physical and Cultural Determinants. American Antiquity 29: 281-300.

Johnson, F. (ed.)
675   1942 The Boylston Street Fishweir. Papers of the R. S. Peabody Foundation for Archaeology 2.

676   1949 The Boylston Street Fishweir II. <u>Papers of the R. S. Peabody Foundation for Archaeology</u> 4(1).

Johnson, F., and H. M. Raup
677   1947 Grassy Island. Archaeological and Botanical Investigations of an Indian Site in the Taunton River, Massachusetts. <u>Papers of the R. S. Peabody Foundation for Archaeology</u> 1(2).

678   1964 Investigations in Southwest Yukon: Geobotanical and Archaeological Reconnaissance. <u>Papers of the R. S. Peabody Foundation for Archaeology</u> 6(1): 1-198.

Johnson, L. J., Jr.
679   1963 Pollen Analysis of Two Archaeological Sites at Amistad Reservoir, Texas. <u>Texas Journal of Science</u> 15: 225-230.

Jones, J. C.
680   1914 The Geologic History of Lake Lahontan. <u>Science</u> 40: 827-830.

681   1925 Geologic History of Lake Lahontan. In, Quaternary Climates. <u>Carnegie Institute of Washington Publication</u> 352: 3-50.

Jones, J. K., Jr.
682   1964 Distribution and Taxonomy of Mammals of Nebraska. <u>University of Kansas Museum of Natural History Publication</u> 16.

Joyce, H.
683   1961 Prehistoric Settlement and Physical Environment in the Mesa Verde Area. <u>University of Utah Anthropological Papers</u> 53.

Judson, S.
684   1946 Late Glacial and Postglacial Chronology on Adak. Journal of Geology 54: 376-385.

685   1949 The Pleistocene Stratigraphy of Boston, Massachusetts and its Relation to the Boylston Street Fishweir. In, F. Johnson (ed.), The Boylston Street Fishweir II. Papers of the R. S. Peabody Foundation for Archaeology 4(1): 7-48.

686   1953 Geology of the San Jon Site, Eastern New Mexico. Smithsonian Miscellaneous Collections 121(1).

Jungerius, P. D.
687   1969 Soil Evidence of Postglacial Tree-Line Fluctuations in the Cypress Hills Area, Alberta, Canada. Arctic and Alpine Research 1: 235-246.

Just, T.
688   1959 Postglacial Vegetation of the North-Central United States: A Review. Journal of Geology 67: 228-238.

Kapp, R. O., and A. M. Gooding
689   1964 A Radiocarbon-Dated Pollen Profile from Sunbeam Prairie Bog, Darke County, Ohio. American Journal of Science 262: 259-299.

Kapp, R. O., and W. A. Kneller
690   1962 A Buried Biotic Assemblage from an Old Saline River Terrace at Milan, Michigan. Papers of the Michigan Academy of Science, Arts and Letters 47: 135-145.

Karlstrom, T. N. V.

691   1953 Upper Cook Inlet Region, Alaska. In, T. L. Péwé, et. al., Multiple Glaciation in Alaska. United States Geological Survey Circular 289: 3-5.

692   1955 Late Pleistocene and Recent Glacial Chronology of South-Central Alaska. Geological Society of America Bulletin 66: 1581-1582.

693   1956 The Problem of the Cochrane in Late Pleistocene Chronology. United States Geological Survey Bulletin 1021-J.

694   1957 Tentative Correlation of Alaskan Glacial Sequences, 1956. Science 125: 73-74.

695   1960 The Cook Inlet, Alaska, Glacial Record and Quaternary Classification. United States Geological Survey Professional Paper 400-B: 330-332.

696   1961 The Glacial History of Alaska: Its Bearing on Paleoclimatic History. New York Academy of Sciences Annals 95: 290-340.

697   1964 Quaternary Geology of the Kenai Lowland and Glacial History of the Cook Inlet Region, Alaska. United States Geological Survey Professional Paper 443.

698   1966 Quaternary Glacial Record of the North Pacific Region and World-Wide Climatic Changes. In, D. I. Blumenstock (ed.), Pleistocene and Post-Pleistocene Climatic Variations in the Pacific, pp. 153-182. Bernice P. Bishop Museum, Honolulu.

Karrow, P. F.
699   1963 Pleistocene Geology of the Hamilton-Galt Area.
      Ontario Department of Mines, Geological Report 16.

Karrow, P. F., J. R. Clark, and J. Terasmae
700   1961 The Age of Lake Iroquois and Lake Ontario.
      Journal of Geology 69: 659-667.

Kauffman, E. G., and D. S. McCulloch
701   1965 Biota of a Late Glacial Rocky Mountain Pond.
      Geological Society of America Bulletin 76: 1203-1232.

Kautz, R. R., and D. H. Thomas
702   1972 Palynological Investigations of Two Prehistoric Cave
      Middens in Central Nevada. Tebiwa 15(2): 43-54.

Kaye, C. A.
703   1962 Early Postglacial Beavers in Southeastern New
      England. Science 138: 906-907.

Kaye, C. A., and E. Barghoorn
704   1964 Late Quaternary Sea-Level Change and Crustal
      Rise at Boston, Massachusetts, with Notes on the
      Auto-compaction of Peat. Geological Society of
      America Bulletin 75: 63-80.

Keen, F. P.
705   1937 Climatic Cycles in Eastern Oregon as Indicated by
      Tree Rings. Monthly Weather Review 65: 175-188.

Kehoe, T. F., and A. B. Kehoe
706   1968 Saskatchewan. In, W. W. Caldwell (ed.), The
      Northwestern Plains: A Symposium. The Center
      for Indian Studies, Occasional Paper 1: 21-35.
      Rocky Mountain College, Billings.

Keller, C. O.
707   1943 A Comparative Study of Three Indiana Bogs. Butler University Botanical Studies 6: 65-80.

Kelley, J. C.
708   1947 The Cultural Affiliation and Chronological Position of the Clear Fork Focus. American Antiquity 13: 97-109.

709   1952 Factors Involved in the Abandonment of Certain Peripheral Southwestern Settlements. American Anthropologist 54: 356-387.

710   1959 The Desert Culture and the Balcones Phase: Archaic Manifestations in the Southwest and Texas. American Antiquity 24: 276-288.

Kelley, J. C., T. N. Campbell, and D. J. Lehmer
711   1940 The Association of Archaeological Materials with Geological Deposits in the Big Bend Region of Texas. Sul Ross State Teacher's College Bulletin 21(3).

Kelso, G.
712   1970 Hogup Cave, Utah: Comparative Pollen Analysis of Human Coprolites and Cave Fill. In, C. M. Aikens, Hogup Cave. University of Utah Anthropological Papers 93: 251-262.

Kendeigh, S. C.
713   1961 Paleo-Ecology: Post-Pleistocene and Summary. In, Animal Ecology, pp. 288-292. Prentice-Hall, Englewood Cliffs.

Kerr, F. A.
714 1936 Quaternary Glaciations in the Coast Range, Northern British Columbia and Alaska. Journal of Geology 44: 681-700.

Kind, N. V.
715 1973 Late Quaternary Climatic Changes and Glacial Events in the Old and New World. Twenty Fourth International Geological Congress, Section 12: 55-61.

Kivett, M. F.
716 1950 Archaeology and Climatic Implications in the Central Plains. In, J. D. Jennings (ed.), Proceedings of the Sixth Plains Archaeological Conference. University of Utah Anthropological Papers 11: 88-89.

Klein, D. R.
717 1965 Postglacial Distribution Patterns of Mammals in the Southern Coastal Ranges of Alaska. Arctic 18: 7-20.

Knox, A. S.
718 1942 The Pollen Analysis of the Silt and the Tentative Dating of the Deposits. In, F. Johnson (ed.), The Boylston Street Fishweir. Papers of the R. S. Peabody Foundation for Archaeology 2: 105-129.

719 1949 Fossil Pollen and Paleoclimatology. American Geophysical Union Transactions 30: 182.

Koerner, R. M., and W. S. B. Paterson
720 1974 Analysis of a Core through the Meighan Ice Cap, Arctic Canada, and its Paleoclimatic Implications. Quaternary Research 4: 253-263.

Kottlowski, F. E., M. E. Cooley, and R. V. Ruhe
721 1965 Quaternary Geology of the Southwest. In, H. E. Wright, Jr., and D. G. Frey (eds.), The Quaternary of the United States, pp. 287-298. Princeton University Press, Princeton.

Kovar, A. J.
722 1965 Pollen Analysis of the Bear Meadows Bog of Central Pennsylvania. Pennsylvania Academy of Science Proceedings 38: 16-24.

723 1967 Report on the Pollen Analysis of the Samples from the Sheep Rock Shelter. In, J. W. Michels and I. F. Smith (eds.), Archaeological Investigations of Sheep Rock Shelter, Huntingdon County, Pennsylvania. Volume I, pp. 85-116. Department of Anthropology, Pennsylvania State University, University Park.

Kramer, F. L.
724 1962 Rivers of Stone. Pacific Discovery 15: 11-15.

Krauss, R. W., and G. N. Kent
725 1944 Analyses and Correlations of Four New Hampshire Bogs. Ohio Journal of Science 44: 11-17.

Krieger, A.
726 1950 A Suggested General Sequence in North American Projectile Points. In, J. D. Jennings (ed.), Proceedings of the Sixth Plains Archaeological Conference. University of Utah Anthropological Papers 11: 117-124.

727 1950 Statement of Problems. In, J. D. Jennings (ed.), Proceedings of the Sixth Plains Archaeological Conference. <u>University of Utah Anthropological Papers</u> 11: 35-39.

728 1952 Review of "The Wheeler Site: A 3500 Year-Old Culture in Dallas County, Texas" by W. W. Crook, Jr., Field and Laboratory 20: 43-65. <u>American Antiquity</u> 18: 183.

729 1961 Review of "Late Pleistocene Environments of North Pacific North America: An Elaboration of Late-Glacial and Post-Glacial Climatic, Physiographic, and Biotic Changes", by C. J. Heusser. <u>American Antiquity</u> 27: 249-250.

Krinsley, D. B.
730 1965 Pleistocene Geology of the Southwest Yukon Territory, Canada. <u>Journal of Glaciology</u> 5: 385-397.

Kupsch, W. O.
731 1960 Radiocarbon-Dated Organic Sediment near Herbert, Saskatchewan. <u>American Journal of Science</u> 258: 282-292.

Kurtén, B., and E. Anderson
732 1972 The Sediments and Fauna of Jaguar Cave: 2-The Fauna. <u>Tebiwa</u> 15(1): 21-45.

Lajoie, K. R.
733 1969 Pleistocene Lacustrine History of Mono Basin, California. <u>Abstracts with Programs for 1969, Part 7</u>: 133. Geological Society of America.

LaMarche, V. C., Jr.
734 1973 Holocene Climatic Variations Inferred from Treeline Fluctuations in the White Mountains, California. Quaternary Research 3: 632-660.

735 1974 Paleoclimatic Inferences from Long Tree-Ring Records. Science 183: 1043-1048.

LaMarche, V. C., Jr., and H. A. Mooney
736 1967 Altithermal Timberline Advance in the Western United States. Nature 213: 980-982.

737 1972 Recent Climatic Change and Development of the Bristlecone Pine (P. longaeva Bailey) Krummholz Zone, Mt. Washington, Nevada. Arctic and Alpine Research 4: 61-72.

Lamb, H. H.
738 1963 On the Nature of Certain Climatic Epochs which Differed from the Modern (1900-1939) Normal. In, Changes of Climate. Proceedings of the WMO/UNESCO Rome 1961 Symposium on Changes of Climate (Arid Zone Research XX), pp. 125-150. UNESCO. (Also in H. H. Lamb, 1966, The Changing Climate, pp. 58-112. Methuen, London).

739 1965 The Early Medieval Warm Epoch and its Sequel. Palaeogeography, Palaeoclimatology, Palaeoecology 1: 13-37.

740 1971 Climates and Circulation Regimes Developed over the Northern Hemisphere during and since the Last Ice Age. Paleogeography, Palaeoclimatology, Palaeoecology 10: 125-162.

741   1972 Atmospheric Circulation and Climate in the Arctic since the Last Ice Age. In, Y. Vasari, H. Hyvärinen, and S. Hicks (eds.), Climatic Changes in Arctic Areas during the Last Ten-Thousand Years. <u>Acta Universitatis Ouluensis, Series A: Scientiae Rerum Naturalium 3, Geologica I: 455-495</u>. University of Oulu, Oulu.

Lamb, H. H., R. P. W. Lewis, and A. Woodroffe
742   1966 Atmospheric Circulation and the Main Climatic Variables between 8000 and 0 B. C.: Meteorological Evidence. In, J. S. Sawyer (ed.), <u>Proceedings of the International Symposium on World Climate 8000 to 0 B. C.</u>, pp. 174-217. Royal Meteorological Society, London.

Lance, J. F.
743   1959 Faunal Remains from the Lehner Mammoth Site. <u>American Antiquity</u> 25: 35-42.

744   1963 Alluvial Stratigraphy in Lake and Moqui Canyons. In, F. W. Sharrock, et. al., 1961 Excavations, Glen Canyon Area. <u>University of Utah Anthropological Papers</u> 63: 347-376.

745   1965 Pleistocene-Holocene Boundary in Southwestern U. S. A. <u>International Association for Quaternary Research, Sixth Congress Report</u>: 439-446.

Lane, G. H.
746   1931 A Preliminary Pollen Analysis of the East McCulloch Peat Bed. <u>Ohio Journal of Science</u> 31: 165-171.

Lange, A. L.
747   1956 Woodchuck Remains in Northern Arizona Caves. <u>Journal of Mammalogy</u> 37: 289-291.

Lasalle, P.
748   1966 Late Quaternary Vegetation and Glacial History in the St. Lawrence Lowlands, Canada. Leidsche Geologische Mededelingen 38: 91-128.

Laudermilk, J. D., and P. A. Munz
749   1934 Plants in the Dung of Nothrotherium from Gypsum Cave, Nevada. Carnegie Institute of Washington Publication 453: 29-38.

750   1938 Plants in the Dung of Nothrotherium from Rampart and Muav Caves, Arizona. Carnegie Institute of Washington Publication 487: 271-282.

Lawrence, D. B.
751   1948 Mt. Hood's Latest Eruption and Glacier Advances. Mazama 39: 22-29.

752   1950 Glacier Fluctuation for Six Centuries in Southeastern Alaska and its Relation to Solar Activity. Geographical Review 40: 191-223.

753   1953 Recession of the Past Two Centuries. In, D. B. Lawrence and J. A. Elson, Periodicity of Deglaciation in North America since the Late-Wisconsin Maximum. Geografiska Annaler 35: 83-94.

754   1958 Glaciers and Vegetation in Southeastern Alaska. American Scientist 46: 88-122.

Layton, T. N.
755   1972 A 12,000 Year Obsidian Hydration Record of Occupation, Abandonment and Lithic Change from the Northwestern Great Basin. Tebiwa 15(2): 22-28.

Lee, T.
756   1957 The Antiquity of the Sheguindah Site. Canadian Field Naturalist 71: 117-137.

Legget, R. F., R. J. E. Brown, and G. H. Johnsston
757   1966 Alluvial Fan Formation near Aklavik, Northwest Territories, Canada. Geological Society of America Bulletin 77: 15-29.

Lehmer, D. J.
758   1970 Climate and Culture History in the Middle Missouri Valley. In, W. Dort, Jr., and J. K. Jones, Jr. (eds.), Pleistocene and Recent Environments of the Central Great Plains. Department of Geology, University of Kansas, Special Publication 3: 117-129.

Lemke, R. W., et. al.
759   1965 Quaternary Geology of Northern Great Plains. In, H. E. Wright, Jr., and D. G. Frey (eds.), The Quaternary of the United States, pp. 15-27. Princeton University Press, Princeton.

Leonhardy, F. C.
760   1966 Late Pleistocene Research at Domebo: A Summary and Interpretation. In, F. Leonhardy (ed.), Domebo: A Paleo-Indian Mammoth Kill in the Prairie-Plains. Contributions of the Museum of the Great Plains 1: 51-53. Lawton.

Leopold, E. B.
761   1956 Two Late-Glacial Deposits in Southern Connecticut. National Academy of Science Proceedings 42: 863-867.

762   1957 Comparisons by Pollen Chronology of Late-Glacial Climate in Eastern U. S. A. with that of the Alleröd in Northern Europe. International Association for Quaternary Research, Fifth Congress, Résumés des Communications: 105-106.

763   1958 Some Aspects of Late-Glacial Climate in Eastern United States. Veröffentlichungen des Geobotanischen Instituts, Eidgenössiche Technische Hochschule Rübel in Zürich 34: 80-85.

764   1967 Late-Cenozoic Patterns of Plant Extinction. In, P. S. Martin and H. E. Wright, Jr., (eds.), Pleistocene Extinctions, pp. 203-246. Yale University Press, New Haven.

Leopold, E. B., and R. A. Scott
765   1958 Pollen and Spores and Their Use in Geology. Smithsonian Institution Report 1957: 303-323.

Leopold, L. B.
766   1951 Pleistocene Climate in New Mexico. American Journal of Science 249: 152-158.

Leopold, L. B., and J. P. Miller
767   1954 A Postglacial Chronology for some Alluvial Valleys in Wyoming. United States Geological Survey Water-Supply Paper 1261: 1-87.

Leopold, L. B., and C. T. Snyder
768   1951 Alluvial Fills near Gallup, New Mexico. United States Geological Survey Water-Supply Paper 1110-A: 1-17.

Leopold, L. B., E. B. Leopold, and F. Wendorf
769   1963 Some Climatic Indicators in the Period A. D. 1200-1400 in New Mexico. In, Changes of Climate. Proceedings of the WMO/UNESCO Rome 1961 Symposium on Changes of Climate (Arid Zone Research XX), pp. 265-270. UNESCO.

Lewis, C. F. M., R. W. Anderson, and A. A. Berti
770   1966 Geological and Palynological Studies of Early Lake Erie Deposits. University of Michigan Great Lakes Research Division Publication 15: 176-191.

Lewis, I. F., and E. C. Cocke
771   1929 Pollen Analysis of Dismal Swamp Peat. Journal of the Elisha Mitchell Scientific Society 45: 37-58.

Lichti-Fedorovich, S., and J. C. Ritchie
772   1968 Recent Pollen Assemblages from the Western Interior of Canada. Review of Palaeobotany and Palynology 7: 297-344.

Lindeman, R. L.
773   1941 The Developmental History of Cedar Creek Bog, Minnesota. American Midland Naturalist 25: 101-112.

Lindsey, A. J.
774   1932 Preliminary Fossil Pollen Analysis of the Merriville, Indiana, White Pine Bog. Butler University Botanical Studies 2: 179-182.

Livingstone, D. A.
775   1955 Some Pollen Profiles from Arctic Alaska. Ecology 36: 587-600.

776 1957 Pollen Analysis of a Valley Fill near Umiat, Alaska. American Journal of Science 255: 254-260.

777 1968 Some Interstadial and Postglacial Pollen Diagrams from Eastern Canada. Ecological Monographs 38: 87-125.

Livingstone, D. A., and A. H. Estes
778 1967 A Carbon-Dated Pollen Diagram from the Cape Breton Plateau, Nova Scotia. Canadian Journal of Botany 45: 339-359.

Livingstone, D. A., and B. G. R. Livingstone
779 1958 Late Glacial and Post Glacial Vegetation from Gillis Lake in Richmond County, Cape Breton Island, Nova Scotia. American Journal of Science 256: 341-359.

Løken, O. H.
780 1962 The Late-Glacial and Postglacial Emergence and the Deglaciation of Northernmost Labrador. Biological Bulletin 17: 23-56.

781 1965 Postglacial Emergence at the South End of Inugsuin Ford, Baffin Island, N. W. T. Geographical Bulletin 7(3-4): 243-258.

Løken, O. H., and J. T. Andrews
782 1966 Glaciology and Chronology of Fluctuations of the Ice Margin at the South End of the Barnes Ice Cap, Baffin Island, N. W. T. Geographical Bulletin 8: 341-359.

Long, C. A.
783   1971 Significance of the Late Pleistocene Fauna from the Little Box Elder Cave, Wyoming, to Studies of Zoogeography of Recent Mammals. Great Basin Naturalist 31: 93-105.

Love, D.
784   1959 The Postglacial Development of the Flora of Manitoba: A Discussion. Canadian Journal of Botany 37: 547-585.

Lueninghoener, G. C.
785   1947 The Post-Kansan Geologic History of the Lower Platte Valley Area. University of Nebraska Studies 2.

Lundelius, E. L., Jr.
786   1962 Nonhuman Skeletal Material from the Kyle Site. In, E. B. Jelks, The Kyle Site: A Stratified Central Texas Aspect Site in Hill County, Texas. University of Texas Department of Anthropology Archaeology Series 5: 111-112.

787   1963 Non-Human Skeletal Material. In, J. F. Epstein, et. al., Centipede and Damp Caves: Excavation in Val Verde County, Texas, 1958. Bulletin of the Texas Archeological Society 33: 127-129.

788   1967 Late-Pleistocene and Holocene Faunal History of Central Texas. In, P. S. Martin and H. E. Wright, Jr., (eds.), Pleistocene Extinctions, pp. 287-319. Yale University Press, New Haven.

Lyons, J. B.
789   1973 Holocene History of a Portion of Northernmost Ellesmere Island. Arctic 26: 314-323.

McAllister, D. E., and S. Qadri
790   1965 Fish Remains from a 2500 Year-Old Lake Superior Archaeological Site, with Notes on Previous Sites. National Museums of Canada Natural History Papers 29.

McAndrews, J. H.
791   1959 A Pollen Diagram from the Site of Glacial Lake Aitkin. Minnesota Academy of Sciences Proceedings 27: 129.

792   1966 Postglacial History of Prairie, Savanna, and Forest in Northwestern Minnesota. Torrey Botanical Club Memoir 22(2).

793   1967 Paleoecology of the Seminary and Mirror Pool Peat Deposits. In, W. J. Mayer-Oakes (ed.), Life, Land and Water, pp. 253-269. University of Manitoba Press, Winnipeg.

794   1967 Pollen Analysis and Vegetational History of the Itasca Region, Minnesota. In, E. J. Cushing and H. E. Wright, Jr. (eds.), Quaternary Paleoecology, pp. 219-236. Yale University Press, New Haven.

795   1968 Pollen Evidence for the Protohistoric Development of the "Big Woods" in Minnesota, U. S. A. Review of Palaeobotany and Palynology 7: 201-211.

796   1969 Paleobotany of a Wild Rice Lake in Minnesota. Canadian Journal of Botany 47: 1671-1679.

McAndrews, J. H., R. E. Stewart, and R. C. Bright
797   1967 Paleoecology of a Prairie Pothole: A Preliminary Report. In, L. Clayton and T. F. Freers (eds.), Glacial Geology of the Missouri Coteau. North Dakota Geological Survey Miscellaneous Series 30: 101-113.

MacClintock, P., and J. Terasmae
798   1960 Glacial History of Covey Hill. Journal of Geology 68: 232-241.

McComb, A. L., and W. E. Loomis
799   1944 Subclimax Prairie. Bulletin of the Torrey Botanical Club 71: 46-76.

McCulloch, D. S.
800   1967 Quaternary Geology of the Alaskan Shore of Chukchi Sea. In, D. M. Hopkins (ed.), The Bering Land Bridge, pp. 91-120. Stanford University Press, Palo Alto.

McCulloch, D. S., and D. M. Hopkins
801   1966 Evidence for an Early Recent Warm Interval in Northwestern Alaska. Geological Society of America Bulletin 77: 1089-1108.

McCulloch, D. S., D. W. Taylor, and M. Rubin
802   1965 Stratigraphy, Non-Marine Mollusks, and Radiometric Dates from Quaternary Deposits in the Kotzebue Sound Area, Western Alaska. Journal of Geology 73: 442-453.

McCulloch, W. F.
803   1930 A Postglacial Forest in Central New York. Ecology 20: 264-271.

MacDonald, G. F.
804   1968 Debert: A Palaeo-Indian Site in Central Nova Scotia. National Museums of Canada Anthropology Papers 16.

McDowell, L. L., et. al.
805   1971 Palynology and Radiocarbon Chronology of Bugbee Wildflower Sanctuary and Natural Area, Caledonia County, Vermont. Pollen et Spores 13: 73-91.

McGhee, R.
806   1970 Speculations on Climatic Change and Thule Culture Development. Folk 11/12: 173-184.

807   1972 Climatic Change and the Development of Canadian Arctic Cultural Traditions. In, S. Vasari, H. Hyvärinen, and S. Hicks (eds.), Climatic Changes in Arctic Areas during the Last Ten-Thousand Years. Acta Universitatis Ouluensis, Series A: Scientiae Rerum Naturalium 3, Geologica 1: 39-60. University of Oulu, Oulu.

MacGinitie, H. D.
808   1958 Climate since the Late Cretaceous. In, C. L. Hubbs (ed.), Zoogeography. American Association for the Advancement of Science Publications 51: 61-79.

Mackay, J. R.
809   1963 The Mackenzie Delta Area, N. W. T. Geographical Branch, Department of Mines and Technical Surveys Memoir 8. Ottawa.

Mackay, J. R., and J. Terasmae
810   1963 Pollen Diagrams in the Mackenzie Delta Area, N. W. T. Arctic 16: 228-238.

MacNeish, R. S.

811   1954 The Pointed Mountain Site near Fort Liard, Northwest Territories, Canada. American Antiquity 19: 234-253.

812   1956 The Engigstciak Site on the Yukon Arctic Coast University of Alaska Anthropological Papers 4(2): 91-111.

813   1959 Men Out of Asia: As Seen from the Northwest Yukon. University of Alaska Anthropological Papers 7(2): 41-70.

814   1964 Investigations in Southwest Yukon: Archaeological Excavation, Comparisons, and Speculation. Papers of the R. S. Peabody Foundation for Archaeology 6: 201-488.

Madole, R. F.

815   1972 Neoglacial Facies in the Colorado Front Range. Arctic and Alpine Research 4: 119-130.

Madsen, D. B.

816   1972 Paleoecological Investigations in Meadow Valley Wash, Nevada. In, D. D. Fowler (ed.), Great Basin Cultural Ecology: A Symposium. Desert Research Institute Publications in the Social Sciences 8: 57-65. University of Nevada, Reno.

Mahaney, W. C.

817   1971 Notes on the "Arikaree Stade" of the Rocky Mountains Neoglacial. Journal of Glaciology 10: 143-144.

818   1972 Audobon: New Name for Colorado Front Range Geological Deposits Formerly Called "Arikaree". Arctic and Alpine Research 4: 355-357.

819   1973 Neoglacial Chronology in the Fourth of July Cirque, Central Colorado Front Range. Geological Society of America Bulletin 84: 161-170.

Maher, L. J., Jr.
820   1964 Ephedra Pollen in Sediments of the Great Lakes Region. Ecology 45: 391-395.

821   1965 Review of "The Last 10,000 Years, A Fossil Pollen Record of the American Southwest" by P. S. Martin. American Journal of Science 263: 191-192.

822   1972 Absolute Pollen Diagram of Redrock Lake, Boulder County, Colorado. Quaternary Research 2: 531-553.

Malde, H. E.
823   1955 Surficial Geology of the Louisville Quadrangle, Colorado. United States Geological Survey Bulletin 996-E.

824   1960 Geological Age of the Claypool Site, Northeastern Colorado. American Antiquity 26: 236-243.

825   1964 Environment and Man in Arid America. Science 145: 123-129.

Malde, H. E., and A. P. Schick
826   1964 Thorne Cave, Northeastern Utah - Geology. American Antiquity 30: 60-73.

Manley, G.
827   1955 A Climatological Survey of the Retreat of the Laurentide Ice Sheet. American Journal of Science 253: 256-273.

828   1966 Problems of the Climatic Optimum: The Contribution of Glaciology. In, J. S. Sawyer (ed.), Proceedings of the International Symposium on World Climate 8000 to 0 B. C., pp. 34-39. Royal Meteorological Society, London.

829   1971 Interpreting the Meteorology of the Late and Post-Glacial. Palaeogeography, Palaeoclimatology, Palaeoecology 10: 163-175.

Martin, P. S(chultz)
830   1957 Pleistocene Biogeography of a Desert Mountain. American Philosophical Society Yearbook 1957: 240-242.

831   1958 Pleistocene Ecology and Biogeography of North America. In, C. L. Hubbs (ed.), Zoogeography. American Association for the Advancement of Science Publications 51: 375-405.

832   1958 Taiga-Tundra and the Full Glacial Period in Chester County, Pennsylvania. American Journal of Science 256: 470-502.

833   1960 Palynology and Prehistory: The Southwest, an Example. Geological Society of America Bulletin 71: 2103.

834   1961 Late Pleistocene Climates in Arid and Tropical North America. International Association for Quaternary Research, Sixth Congress, Abstracts of Papers: Supplement, pp. 32-33.

835   1961 Southwestern Animal Communities in the Late Pleistocene. In, L. M. Shields and L. J. Gardner (eds.), Bioecology of the Arid and Semiarid Lands of the Southwest. New Mexico Highlands University Bulletin 212: 56-66.

836   1962 On Attempting to Explain the Post-13th Century Pine Rise. Pollen et Spores 4: 364.

837   1963 Early Man in Arizona; The Pollen Evidence. American Antiquity 29: 67-73.

838   1963 The Last 10,000 Years. University of Arizona Press, Tucson.

839   1965 Pollen Analysis in the Glen Canyon. In, F. W. Sharrock, et. al., 1962 Excavations, Glen Canyon Area. University of Utah Anthropological Papers 73: 177-195.

840   1967 Prehistoric Overkill. In, P. S. Martin and H. E. Wright, Jr. (eds.), Pleistocene Extinctions, pp. 75-120. Yale University Press, New Haven.

Martin, P. S(chultz) and W. Byers
841   1965 Pollen and Archaeology at Wetherill Mesa. Society for American Archaeology Memoir 19: 122-135.

Martin, P. S(chultz) and J. Gray
842   1962 Pollen Analysis and the Cenozoic. Science 137: 103-111.

Martin, P. S(chultz) and P. J. Mehringer, Jr.
843   1965 Pleistocene Pollen Analysis and Biogeography of the Southwest. In, H. E. Wright, Jr., and D. G. Frey (eds.), The Quaternary of the United States, pp. 433-451. Princeton University Press, Princeton.

Martin, P. S(chultz) and J. Schoenwetter
844   1960 Arizona's Oldest Cornfield. Science 132: 33-34.

Martin, P. S(chultz), B. Sabels, and D. Shutler
845   1961 Rampart Cave Coprolite and Ecology of the Shasta Ground Sloth. American Journal of Science 259: 102-127.

Martin, P. S(idney) and F. Plog
846   1973 The Archaeology of Arizona. Doubleday/Natural History Press, New York.

Martin, P. S(idney), J. B. Rinaldo, and E. Antevs
847   1949 Cochise and Mogollon Sites, Pine Lawn Valley, Western New Mexico. Chicago Natural History Museum, Fieldiana (Anthropology) 38: 1-232.

Martin, P. S(idney), et. al.
848   1956 Higgins Flat Pueblo, Western New Mexico. Chicago Natural History Museum, Fieldiana (Anthropology) 45.

849   1962 Chapters in the Pre-History of Eastern Arizona, I. Chicago Natural History Museum, Fieldiana (Anthropology) 53.

Marwitt, J. F., G. F. Fry, and J. M. Adovasio
850   1971 Sandwich Shelter. In, C. M. Aikens (ed.), Great Basin Anthropological Conference 1970: Selected Papers. University of Oregon Anthropological Papers 1: 27-36.

Mason, R. J.
851 1958 Late Pleistocene Geochronology and Paleo-Indian Penetration into the Lower Michigan Peninsula. <u>Museum of Anthropology, University of Michigan, Anthropological Papers</u> 11.

Matson, R. G.
852 1972 Pollen from the Spring Garden Ravine Site (4-Pla-101). In, E. W. Ritter and P. D. Schulz (eds.), Papers on Nisenan Environment and Subsistence. <u>Center for Archaeological Research at Davis, Publication</u> 3: 24-27.

Matteson, M. R.
853 1960 Reconstruction of Prehistoric Environments through the Analysis of Molluscan Collections from Shell Middens. <u>American Antiquity</u> 26: 117-120.

Matthes, F. E.
854 1932 Annual Reports of Permanent Committees for 1931-1932: On Glaciers. <u>American Geophysical Union Transactions</u> 13: 282-287.

855 1935 Why We Should Measure Our Glaciers. <u>Sierra Club Bulletin</u> 20: 20-27.

856 1939 Report of Committee on Glaciers, April 1939. <u>American Geophysical Union Transactions</u> 20: 518-523.

857 1939 The Glaciers of Our Own Time. <u>Mazama</u> 21: 20-26.

858 1940 Report of Committee on Glaciers, 1939-40. <u>American Geophysical Union Transactions</u> 21: 396-406.

859   1941 Rebirth of Glaciers of the Sierra Nevada during Late Post-Pleistocene Time. Geological Society of America Bulletin 52: 2030.

860   1942 Glaciers. In, O. E. Meinzer (ed.), Hydrology, pp. 149-219. McGraw-Hill, New York.

861   1942 Report of Committee on Glaciers, 1941-1942. American Geophysical Union Transactions 23: 374-392.

862   1943 Report of Committee on Glaciers, 1942-43. American Geophysical Union Transactions 24: 389-401.

863   1945 Post-Pleistocene Deglaciation and Reglaciation. Geological Society of America Bulletin 56: 1181.

864   1946 How Old are the Moraines on Mt. Hood? Mazama 28: 73-76.

865   1948 Moraines with Ice Cores in the Sierra Nevada. Sierra Club Bulletin 33: 87-96.

866   1950 The Little Ice Age. In, F. Fryxell (ed.), The Incomparable Valley, Chapter 9. University of California Press, Berkeley.

Matthews, B.

867   1967 Late Quaternary Land Emergence in Northern Ungava, Quebec. Arctic 20: 176-202.

868   1967 Late Quaternary Marine Fossils from Frobisher Bay (Baffin Island, N. W. T., Canada). Palaeogeography, Palaeoclimatology, Palaeoecology 3: 243-263.

Matthews, J. V., Jr.
869   1970 Quaternary Environmental History of Interior Alaska: Pollen Samples from Organic Colluvium and Peats. Arctic and Alpine Research 2: 241-251.

Matthews, W. H.
870   1951 Historic and Prehistoric Fluctuations of Alpine Glaciers in the Mount Garibaldi Map-Area, Southwestern British Columbia. Journal of Geology 59: 357-380.

Mawby, J. E.
871   1967 Fossil Vertebrates of the Tule Springs Area. In, H. M. Wormington and D. Ellis (eds.), Pleistocene Studies in Southern Nevada. Nevada State Museum Anthropological Papers 13: 105-129.

Maxwell, J. A., and M. B. Davis
872   1972 Pollen Evidence of Pleistocene and Holocene Vegetation on the Allegheny Plateau, Maryland. Quaternary Research 2: 506-530.

Maycock, P. F., and B. Matthews
873   1966 An Arctic Forest in the Tundra of Northern Ungava. Arctic 19: 114-144.

Mehringer, P. J., Jr.
874   1964 Late Pleistocene Vegetation in the Mohave Desert of Southern Nevada. Geochronology Laboratories, University of Arizona, Interim Research Report 6.

875   1965 Late Pleistocene Vegetation in the Mohave Desert of Southern Nevada. Arizona Academy of Science Journal 3: 172-188.

876 1966 Some Notes on the Late Quaternary Biogeography of the Mohave Desert. Geochronology Laboratories, University of Arizona, Interim Research Report II.

877 1967 Late Quaternary Vegetation in the Mohave Desert (U. S. A.). Review of Palaeobotany and Palynology 2: 319-320.

878 1967 Pollen Analysis and the Alluvial Chronology. Kiva 32: 96-101.

879 1967 Pollen Analysis of the Tule Springs Area. In, H. M. Wormington and D. Ellis (eds.), Pleistocene Studies in Southern Nevada. Nevada State Museum Anthropological Papers 13: 129-200.

880 1967 The Environment of Extinction of the Late-Pleistocene Megafauna in the Arid Southwestern United States. In, P. S. Martin and H. E. Wright, Jr. (eds.), Pleistocene Extinctions, pp. 247-266. Yale University Press, New Haven.

Mehringer, P. J., Jr., and C. W. Ferguson
881 1969 Pluvial Occurrence of Bristlecone Pine (Pinus aristata) in a Mohave Desert Mountain Range. Department of Geochronology, University of Arizona, Interim Research Report 14.

Mehringer, P. J., Jr., and C. V. Haynes, Jr.
882 1965 The Pollen Evidence for the Environment of Early Man and Extinct Animals at the Lehner Mammoth Site, Southeastern Arizona. American Antiquity 31: 17-23.

Mehringer, P. J., Jr., J. E. King, and E. H. Lindsay
883   1970 A Record of Wisconsin-Age Vegetation and Fauna from the Ozarks of Western Missouri. In, W. Dort, Jr., and J. K. Jones, Jr., (eds.), Pleistocene and Recent Environments of the Central Great Plains. Department of Geology, University of Kansas, Special Publication 3: 173-183.

Mehringer, P. J., Jr., P. S. Martin, and C. V. Haynes, Jr.
884   1966 Murray Springs, A Mid-Postglacial Pollen Profile from Southeastern Arizona. Geochronology Laboratories, University of Arizona, Interim Research Report 13.

885   1967 Murray Springs, A Mid-Postglacial Pollen Record from Southern Arizona. American Journal of Science 265: 786-797.

Mehringer, P. J., Jr., et. al.
886   1968 Late-Pleistocene Boreal Forest in the Western Ozarks Highlands? Ecology 49: 567-568.

Meier, M. F.
887   1964 The Recent History of Advance-Retreat and Net Budget of South Cascade Glacier. American Geophysical Union Transactions 45: 608.

Meighan, C. W.
888   1965 Pacific Coast Archaeology. In, H. E. Wright, Jr., and D. G. Frey (eds.), The Quaternary of the United States, pp. 709-720. Princeton University Press, Princeton.

Melton, F. A.
889 1940 A Tentative Classification of Sand Dunes - Its Application to Dune History in the Southern High Plains. Journal of Geology 48: 113-174.

Mercer. J. H.
890 1956 Geomorphology and Glacial History of Southernmost Baffin Island. Geological Society of America Bulletin 67: 553-570.

891 1972 The Lower Boundary of the Holocene. Quaternary Research 2: 15-24.

Miller, C. D.
892 1969 Chronology of Neoglacial Moraines in the Dome Peak Area, North Cascade Range, Washington. Arctic and Alpine Research 1: 49-66.

Miller, G. H.
893 1973 Late Quaternary Glacial and Climatic History of Northern Cumberland Peninsula, Baffin Island, N. W. T., Canada. Quaternary Research 3: 561-583.

Miller, J. P.
894 1958 Problems of the Pleistocene in Cordilleran North America, as Related to Reconstruction of Environmental Changes that Affected Early Man. In, T. L. Smiley (ed.), Climate and Man in the Southwest. University of Arizona Bulletin 28(4): 19-49.

Miller, J. P., and F. Wendorf
895 1958 Alluvial Chronology of the Tesuque Valley, New Mexico. Journal of Geology 66: 177-194.

Miller, N. G.

896   1970 Late and Post-Glacial Vegetation Change in Southwestern New York State. New York Glaciogram 4(2): 7-10.

897   1973 Late-Glacial and Postglacial Vegetation Change in Southwestern New York. New York State Museum and Science Service Bulletin 420.

Miller, N. G., and W. S. Benninghoff

898   1969 Plant Fossils from a Cary-Port Huron Interstade Deposit and Their Paleoecological Interpretation. Geological Society of America Special Paper 123: 225-248.

Miller, R. R.

899   1955 Fish Remains from Archaeological Sites in the Lower Colorado River Basin, Arizona. Papers of the Michigan Academy of Science, Arts and Letters 40: 125-135.

Moir, D. R.

900   1957 An Occurrence of Buried Coniferous Wood in the Altamont Moraine in North Dakota. North Dakota Academy of Science Proceedings 11: 1-5.

901   1958 Occurrence and Radiocarbon Date of Coniferous Wood in Kidder County, North Dakota. North Dakota Geological Survey Miscellaneous Series 10: 108-114.

Moir, W. H., J. F. Franklin, and C. Maser
902   1973 Lost Forest Research Natural Area. In, J. F. Franklin, et. al., Federal Research Natural Areas in Oregon and Washington: A Guidebook for Scientists and Educators, Supplement 3. United States Department of Agriculture Forest Service, Pacific Northwest Forest and Range Experiment Station, Portland.

Moore, G. W.
903   1956 Aragonite Speliothems as Indicators of Paleotemperatures. American Journal of Science 254: 746-753.

Mörner, N. -A.
904   1971 Eustatic and Climatic Oscillations. Arctic and Alpine Research 3: 167-171.

905   1973 World Climate during the Last 130,000 Years. Twenty Fourth International Geological Congress, Section 12: 72-79.

Morrison, A.
906   1970 Pollen Diagrams from Interior Labrador. Canadian Journal of Botany 48: 1957-1975.

Morrison, R. B.
907   1961 A Suggested Pleistocene-Recent (Holocene) Boundary for the Great Basin Region, Nevada-Utah. United States Geological Survey Professional Paper 424-D: 115-116.

908 1961 Correlation of the Deposits of Lakes Lahontan and Bonneville and the Glacial Sequences of the Sierra Nevada and Wasatch Mountains, California, Nevada, and Utah. United States Geological Survey Professional Paper 424-D: 122-124.

909 1961 Lake Lahontan Stratigraphy and History in the Carson Desert (Fallon) Area, Nevada. United States Geological Survey Professional Paper 424-D: 111-114.

910 1964 Lake Lahontan: Geology of Southern Carson Desert, Nevada. United States Geological Survey Professional Paper 401.

911 1965 Lake Bonneville: Quaternary Stratigraphy of Eastern Jordan Valley, South of Salt Lake City, Utah. United States Geological Survey Professional Paper 477.

912 1965 Quaternary Geology of the Great Basin. In, H. E. Wright, Jr., and D. G. Frey (eds.), The Quaternary of the United States, pp. 265-285. Princeton University Press, Princeton.

Morrison, R. B., and J. C. Frye
913 1965 Correlation of the Middle and Late Quaternary Successions of the Lake Lahontan, Lake Bonneville, Rocky Mountain (Wasatch Range), Southern Great Plains, and Eastern Midwest Areas. Nevada Bureau of Mines Report 9. (Reprinted as Illinois Geological Survey Reprint Series 1965-0, 1965).

Morrison, R. B., et. al.
914   1957 In Behalf of the Recent. American Journal of Science 255: 385-393.

Moss, B. W.
915   1940 A Comparative Pollen Analysis of Two Bogs within the Boundaries of Late Wisconsin Glaciation in Indiana. Butler University Botanical Studies 4: 207-216.

Moss, J. H.
916   1951 Glaciation in the Wind River Mountains and its Relation to Early Man in the Eden Valley. In, J. H. Moss, et. al., Early Man in the Eden Valley, pp. 5-92. University of Pennsylvania Monographs.

Muller, E. H.
917   1953 Northern Alaska Peninsula and Eastern Kilbuck Mountains, Alaska. In, T. L. Péwé, et. al., Multiple Glaciation in Alaska. United States Geological Survey Circular 289: 2-3.

Müller, F.
918   1962 Analysis of some Stratigraphic Observations and Radiocarbon Dates from Two Pingos in the Mackenzie Delta Area, N. W. T. Arctic 15: 278-288.

919   1966 Evidence of Climatic Fluctuations on Axel Heiberg Island, Canadian Arctic Archipelago. In, J. O. Fletcher (ed.), Proceedings of the Symposium on the Arctic Heat Budget and Atmospheric Circulation, pp. 135-156. Memorandum RM-5233-NSF. Rand Corporation, Santa Monica.

Murray, K. F.
920   1957 Pleistocene Climate and the Fauna of Burnet Cave, New Mexico. Ecology 38: 129-132.

Nance, C. R.
921   1972 Cultural Evidence for the Altithermal in Texas and Mexico. Southwestern Journal of Anthropology 28: 169-192.

Napton, L. K., et. al.
922   1969 Archaeological and Paleobiological Investigations in Lovelock Cave, Nevada. Kroeber Anthropological Society Papers, Special Publication 2.

Neill, W. T., H. J. Gut, and P. Brodkorb
923   1956 Animal Remains from Four Preceramic Sites in Florida. American Antiquity 21: 383-395.

Nelson, R. L.
924   1954 Glacial Geology of the Frying Pan Drainage, Colorado. Journal of Geology 62: 325-343.

Newman, T. N.
925   1966 Cascadia Cave. Occasional Papers of the Idaho State University Museum 19.

Nichols, D. R.
926   1966 Permafrost in the Recent Epoch. Proceedings of the International Permafrost Conference. National Academy of Sciences-National Research Council Publication 1287: 172-175.

Nichols, H.

927   1965 Climate and Post-Glacial Forest History in Southwestern Keewatin, N. W. T.: II. Palynological Evidence. International Association for Quaternary Research, Seventh Congress, General Services Abstracts: 361.

928   1967 Central Canadian Palynology and its Relevance to Northwestern Europe in the Late Quaternary Period. Review of Palaeobotany and Palynology 2: 231-243.

929   1967 Pollen Diagrams from Subarctic Central Canada. Science 155: 1665-1668.

930   1967 The Post-Glacial History of Vegetation and Climate at Ennadai Lake, Keewatin, and Lynn Lake, Manitoba (Canada). Eiszeitalter und Gegenwart 18: 176-197.

931   1968 Pollen Analysis, Paleotemperatures, and the Summer Position of the Arctic Front in the Postglacial History of Keewatin, Canada. American Meteorological Society Bulletin 49: 387-388.

932   1969 Chronology of Peat Growth in Canada. Palaeogeography, Palaeoclimatology, Palaeoecology 6: 61-65.

933   1969 The Late Quaternary History of Vegetation and Climate at Porcupine Mountain and Clearwater Bog, Manitoba. Arctic and Alpine Research 1: 155-167.

934   1970 Late Quaternary Pollen Diagrams from the Canadian Arctic Barren Grounds at Pelly Lake, Northern Keewatin, N. W. T. Arctic and Alpine Research 2: 43-61.

935   1972 Summary of the Palynological Evidence for Late-Quaternary Vegetational and Climatic Change in the Central and Eastern Canadian Arctic. In, Y. Vasari, H. Hyvärinen and S. Hicks (eds.), Climatic Changes in Arctic Areas during the Last Ten-Thousand Years. Acta Universitatis Ouluensis, Series A: Scientiae Rerum Naturalium 3, Geologica 1: 309-339. University of Oulu, Oulu.

Niering, W. A.
936   1953 The Past and Present Vegetation of High Point State Park, New Jersey. Ecological Monographs 23: 127-148.

O'Bryan, D.
937   1952 The Abandonment of the Northern Pueblos in the Thirteenth Century. In, S. Tax (ed.), Indian Tribes of North America. Selected Papers of the Twenty Ninth International Congress of Americanists, pp. 153-157. University of Chicago Press, Chicago.

O'Connell, J. F., and P. S. Hayward
938   1972 Altithermal and Medithermal Human Adaptations in Surprise Valley, Northeast California. In, D. D. Fowler (ed.), Great Basin Cultural Ecology: A Symposium. Desert Research Institute Publications in the Social Sciences 8: 25-41. University of Nevada, Reno.

Ogden, J. G., III

939   1958 Problems of Tundra Interpretation and New England Late-Glacial Diagrams. Ecological Society of America Bulletin 39: 114-115.

940   1959 A Late-Glacial Pollen Sequence from Martha's Vineyard, Massachusetts. American Journal of Science 257: 366-381.

941   1960 Recurrence Surfaces and Pollen Stratigraphy of a Postglacial Raised Bog, Kings County, Nova Scotia. American Journal of Science 258: 341-353.

942   1961 Forest History of Martha's Vineyard, Massachusetts. I. Modern and Pre-Colonial Forests. American Midland Naturalist 66: 417-430.

943   1963 The Squibnocket Cliff Site; Radiocarbon Dates and Pollen Stratigraphy. American Journal of Science 261: 344-353.

944   1965 Great Lakes-Ohio River Valley. International Association for Quaternary Research, Seventh Congress, Guidebook G: Day 9, Stop 9.6, p. 79.

945   1965 Pleistocene Pollen Records from Eastern North America. Botanical Review 31: 481-504.

946   1966 Forest History of Ohio. I. Radiocarbon Dates and Pollen Stratigraphy of Silver Lake, Logan County, Ohio. Ohio Journal of Science 66: 387-400.

947   1967 Radiocarbon and Pollen Evidence for a Sudden Change in Climate in the Great Lakes Region Approximately 10,000 Years Ago. In, E. J. Cushing and H. E. Wright, Jr., (eds.), Quaternary Paleoecology, pp. 117-127. Yale University Press, New Haven.

948   1969 Correlation of Contemporary and Late Pleistocene Pollen Records in the Reconstruction of Postglacial Environments in Northeastern North America. Mitteilungen Internationale Vereinigung für Theoretische und Angewandte Limnologie 17: 64-77.

Ogden, J. G., III, and R. J. Hay
949   1967 Ohio Wesleyan University Radiocarbon Measurements III. Radiocarbon 9: 316-332.

Oldfield, F., and J. Schoenwetter
950   1964 Late Quaternary Environments and Early Man on the Southern High Plains. Antiquity 38: 226-229.

Oliver, J. L.
951   1951 Forest Succession in the Valparaiso and Packerton Moraines in Indiana. Butler University Botanical Studies 10: 20-28.

Oltz, D. F., Jr., and R. O. Kapp
952   1963 Plant Remains Associated with Mastodon and Mammoth Remains in Central Michigan. American Midland Naturalist 70: 339-346.

Orr, P. C.
953   1956 Pleistocene Man in Fishbone Cave, Pershing County, Nevada. Nevada State Museum Department of Archaeology Bulletin 2: 1-20.

Osborne, D.
954   1953 Archaeological Occurrence of Pronghorn Antelope, Bison, and Horse in the Columbia Plateau. Scientific Monthly 77: 260-269.

Osborne, D., et. al.
955   1967 The Dendrochronology of the Wetherill Mesa Archaeological Project. Tree-Ring Bulletin 28: 1-40.

Osvald, H.
956   1935 A Bog at Hartford, Michigan. Ecology 16: 520-528.

957   1936 Stratigraphy and Pollen Flora of some Bogs of the North Pacific Coast of America. Schweizerische Botanische Gesellschaft 46: 489-504.

Oswalt, W. H.
958   1957 Volcanic Activity and Alaskan Spruce Growth in A. D. 1783. Science 126: 928-929.

Otto, J. H.
959   1938 Forest Succession in the Southern Limits of Early Wisconsin Glaciation as Indicated by a Pollen Spectrum from Bacon's Swamp, Marion County, Indiana. Butler University Botanical Studies 4: 93-116.

Outcalt, S. I., and D. D. MacPhail
960   1965 A Survey of Neoglaciation in the Front Range of Colorado. University of Colorado Studies, Series in Earth Sciences 4.

Parmalee, P. W.

961 1959 Animal Remains from the Modoc Rock Shelter Site, Randolph County, Illinois. Appendix II in, M. L. Fowler (ed.), Summary Report of Modoc Rock Shelter, 1952, 1953, 1955, 1956. Illinois State Museum Report of Investigations 8: 61-65.

962 1967 A Recent Cave Bone Deposit in Southwestern Illinois. National Speleological Society Bulletin 29: 119-147.

963 1968 Cave and Archaeological Faunal Deposits as Indicators of Post-Pleistocene Animal Populations and Distribution in Illinois. In, R. E. Bergstrom (ed.), The Quaternary of Illinois. University of Illinois College of Agriculture Special Publication 14: 104-113.

964 1970 Birds from Hogup Cave. In, C. M. Aikens, Hogup Cave. University of Utah Anthropological Papers 93: 263-266.

Parmalee, P. W., and D. F. Hoffmeister

965 1957 Archaeo-zoological Evidence of the Spotted Skunk in Illinois. Journal of Mammalogy 38: 261.

Parmalee, P. W., and R. D. Oesch

966 1972 Pleistocene and Recent Faunas from the Brynjulfson Caves, Missouri. Illinois State Museum Report of Investigations 25.

Parmalee, P. W., R. A. Bieri, and R. K. Mohrman

967 1961 Mammal Remains from an Illinois Cave. Journal of Mammalogy 42: 119.

Patrick, R.
968 1943 The Diatoms of Linsley Pond, Connecticut. <u>Academy of Natural Sciences of Philadelphia Proceedings</u> 95: 53-110.

969 1946 Diatoms from Patschke Bog, Texas. <u>Academy of Natural Sciences of Philadelphia, Notulae Naturae</u> 170.

Patton, T. H.
970 1963 Fossil Vertebrates from Miller's Cave, Llano County, Texas. <u>Texas Memorial Museum Bulletin</u> 7.

Pennak, R. W.
971 1963 Ecological and Radiocarbon Correlations in some Colorado Mountain Lake and Bog Deposits. <u>Ecology</u> 44: 1-15.

Péwé, T. L.
972 1951 Recent History of Black Rapids Glacier, Alaska. <u>Geological Society of America Bulletin</u> 62: 1558.

973 1953 Big Delta Area, Alaska. In, T. L. Péwé, et. al., Multiple Glaciation in Alaska. <u>United States Geological Survey Circular</u> 289: 8-10.

974 1954 The Geological Approach to Dating Archaeological Sites. <u>American Antiquity</u> 20: 51-61.

975 1957 Recent History of Canwell and Castner Glaciers, Alaska. <u>Geological Society of America Bulletin</u> 68: 1779.

976   1961 Multiple Glaciation in the Headwaters Area of the Delta River, Central Alaska. United States Geological Survey Professional Paper 424-D: 200-201.

977   1965 Résumé of Quaternary Geology of the Delta River Area, Alaska Range. International Association for Quaternary Research, Seventh Congress, Guidebook for Field Conference F, Central and South Central Alaska, pp. 55-93.

978   1965 Résumé of Quaternary Geology of the Fairbanks Area. International Association for Quaternary Research, Seventh Congress, Guidebook F, Central and South Alaska, pp. 6-36.

979   1967 Permafrost and its Effect on Life in the North. In, H. P. Hansen (ed.), Arctic Biology, pp. 27-65. Oregon State University Press, Corvallis.

Péwé, T. L., D. M. Hopkins, and J. L. Giddings, Jr.
980   1965 The Quaternary Geology and Archaeology of Alaska. In, H. E. Wright, Jr., and D. G. Frey (eds.), The Quaternary of the United States, pp. 355-374. Princeton University Press, Princeton.

Péwé, T. L., et. al.
981   1953 Multiple Glaciation in Alaska. United States Geological Survey Circular 289.

982   1953 Tentative Correlation of Glaciations in Alaska. In, T. L. Péwé, et. al., Multiple Glaciation in Alaska. United States Geological Survey Circular 289: 12-13.

Pheasant, D. J., and J. T. Andrews
983   1973 The Quaternary History of the Northern Cumberland Peninsula, Baffin Island, N. W. T.: Part VIII, Chronology of Narpaing and Quajon Fiords during the Past 120,000 Years. <u>Twenty Fourth International Geological Congress</u>, Section 12: 81-88.

Phleger, F. B.
984   1949 The Foraminifera. In, F. Johnson (ed.), The Boylston Street Fishweir II. <u>Papers of the R. S. Peabody Foundation for Archaeology</u> 4(1): 99-108.

Plafker, G., and D. J. Miller
985   1957 Recent History of Glaciation in the Malaspina District and Adjoining Bays, Alaska. <u>Geological Society of America Bulletin</u> 68: 1909.

986   1958 Glacial Features and Surficial Deposits of the Malaspina District, Alaska. <u>United States Geological Survey Miscellaneous Investigations Map I-271</u>.

987   1958 Recent History of Glaciation in the Malaspina District and Adjoining Bays, Alaska. <u>Geological Society of America Bulletin</u> 69: 1700.

Porsild, A. E.
988   1938 Earth Mounds in Unglaciated Arctic Northwestern North America. <u>Geographical Review</u> 28: 46-58.

Porsild, M. P.
989   1922 The Flora of Greenland: Its Affinities and Probable Age and Origin. <u>Torreya</u> 22: 53-54.

Porter, S. C.
990 1964 Late Pleistocene Glacial Chronology of North-Central Brooks Range, Alaska. American Journal of Science 262: 446-460.

991 1966 Pleistocene Geology of Anaktuvuk Pass, Central Brooks Range, Alaska. Arctic Institute of North America, Technical Paper 18.

992 1971 Fluctuations of Late Pleistocene Alpine Glaciers in Western North America. In, K. K. Turekian (ed.), The Late Cenozoic Glacial Ages, pp. 307-330. Yale University Press, New Haven.

Porter, S. C., and G. H. Denton
993 1967 Chronology of Neoglaciation in the North American Cordillera. American Journal of Science 265: 177-210.

Potter, L. D.
994 1947 Postglacial Forest Sequence of North-Central Ohio. Ecology 28: 396-417.

Potzger, J. E.
995 1932 Succession of Forests as Indicated by Fossil Pollen from a Northern Michigan Bog. Science 75: 366.

996 1936 Post-Glacial Fossil Records in Peat of the Upper Blue River Valley, Henry County, Indiana. Indiana Academy of Science Proceedings 45: 64-68.

997 1942 Pollen Profile from an Extinct Lake in Hendricks County, Indiana, Marks Time of Drainage. Indiana Academy of Science Proceedings 52: 83-86.

998   1942 Pollen Spectra from Four Bogs on the Gillen Nature Reserve along the Michigan-Wisconsin State Line. American Midland Naturalist 28: 501-511.

999   1943 Pollen Study of Five Bogs in Price and Sawyer Counties, Wisconsin. Butler University Botanical Studies 6: 54-64.

1000   1944 Pollen Frequency of Abies and Picea in Peat: A Correction on some Published Records from Indiana Bogs and Lakes. Butler University Botanical Studies 6: 123-130.

1001   1945 The Pine Barrens of New Jersey, a Refugium during Pleistocene Times. Butler University Botanical Studies 7: 182-196.

1002   1946 A Pollen Study in the Tension Zone in the Saginaw, Michigan Area of Lower Michigan. Indiana Academy of Science Proceedings 56: 35.

1003   1946 Phytosociology of the Primeval Forest in Central-Northern Wisconsin and Upper Michigan and a Brief Post-Glacial History of the Lake Forest Formation. Ecological Monographs 16: 211-250.

1004   1948 A Pollen Study in the Tension Zone of Lower Michigan. Butler University Botanical Studies 8: 161-177.

1005   1950 Bogs of the Quetico-Superior Country Tell its Forest History. Special Bulletin, Butler University Botanical Laboratories Contribution 235.

1006   1951 The Fossil Record near the Glacial Border. Ohio Journal of Science 51: 126-133.

1007   1952 What Can Be Inferred from Pollen Profiles of Bogs of the New Jersey Pine Barrens. Bartonia 26: 20-27.

1008   1953 History of Forest in Quetico-Superior Country from Fossil Pollen Studies. Journal of Forestry 51: 560-565.

1009   1953 Nineteen Bogs from Southern Quebec. Canadian Journal of Botany 31: 383-401.

1010   1954 Comparison of Forest Chronology from a Peat Layer Exposed by Wave Action with a Deep Inland Bog. Ecological Society of America Bulletin 35: 65-66.

1011   1954 Post-Algonquin and Post-Nipissing Forest History of Isle Royale, Michigan. Butler University Botanical Studies 11: 200-209.

1012   1956 Pollen Profiles as Indicators in the History of Lake Filling and Bog Formation. Ecology 37: 476-483.

1013   1956 Series of Bogs across Quebec from the St. Lawrence Valley to James Bay. Canadian Journal of Botany 34: 473-500.

1014   1957 Pollen Study in the Gatineau Valley, Quebec. Bulletin de Service de Biogéographie 17: 12-23.

Potzger, J. E., and A. Courtemanche

1015   1954 A Radiocarbon Date of Peat from James Bay in Quebec. Science 119: 908.

1016   1954 Bog and Lake Studies on the Laurentian Shield in Mont Tremblant Park, Quebec. Canadian Journal of Botany 32: 549-560.

1017   1956 Pollen Study in the Gatineau Valley, Quebec. Butler University Botanical Studies 13: 12-23.

Potzger, J. E., and R. Friesner

1018   1939 Plant Migrations in the Southern Limits of Wisconsin Glaciation in Indiana. American Midland Naturalist 22: 351-368.

1019   1948 Forests of the Past along the Coast of Southern Maine. Butler University Botanical Studies 8: 178-203.

Potzger, J. E., and C. O. Keller

1020   1943 Post-Glacial Records from Four Bogs along the Southern Border of Vilas County, Wisconsin. Transactions of the Wisconsin Academy of Sciences, Arts and Letters 35: 147-156.

Potzger, J. E., and J. H. Otto

1021   1943 Post-Glacial Forest Succession in Northern New Jersey as Shown by Pollen Records from Five Bogs. American Journal of Botany 30: 83-87.

Potzger, J. E., and R. R. Richards

1022   1942 Forest Succession in the Trout Lake, Vilas County, Wisconsin Area: A Pollen Study. Butler University Botanical Studies 5: 179-189.

Potzger, J. E., and B. C. Tharp
1023   1943 Pollen Records of Canadian Spruce and Fir from Texas Bog. Science 98: 584.

1024   1947 Pollen Profile from a Texas Bog. Ecology 28: 274-280.

1025   1954 Pollen Study of Two Bogs in Texas. Ecology 35: 462-466.

Potzger, J. E., and I. T. Wilson
1026   1941 Post-Pleistocene Forest Migration as Indicated by Sediments from Three Deep Inland Lakes. American Midland Naturalist 25: 270-289.

Prettyman, R. L.
1027   1937 Fossil Pollen Analysis of Fox Prairie Bog, Hamilton County, Indiana. Butler University Botanical Studies 4: 33-42.

Pruitt, W. O.
1028   1954 Additional Animal Remains from under Sleeping Bear Dune, Leelanau County, Michigan. Papers of the Michigan Academy of Science, Arts and Letters 39: 253-256.

Putnam, W. C.
1029   1949 Quaternary Geology of the June Lake District, California. Geological Society of America Bulletin 60: 1281-1302.

1030   1950 Moraine and Shoreline Relationships at Mono Lake, California. Geological Society of America Bulletin 61: 115-122.

Quimby, G. I.

1031   1954 Cultural and Natural Areas before Kroeber. American Antiquity 19: 317-331.

1032   1954 The Old Copper Assemblage and Extinct Animals. American Antiquity 20: 169-170.

1033   1957 Dating the Past - Upper Great Lakes Area. Chicago Natural History Museum Bulletin 28(6): 6-7.

1034   1962 Omaha Kinship Terminology and Spruce-Fir Pollen. American Antiquity 28: 91-92.

Quinn, J. H.

1035   1973 Extinct Mammals in Arkansas and Related C14 Dates Circa 3000 Years Ago. Twenty Fourth International Geological Congress, Section 12: 89-96.

Radforth, N. W.

1036   1945 Report on the Pollen and Spore Constituents of a Peat Bed in the Shipsaw Area, Quebec. Royal Society of Canada Transactions, Series 3, Section 5: 131-142.

Rahm, D. A.

1037   1964 Glacial Geology of the Bishop Area, Sierra Nevada, California. Geological Society of America Special Paper 76 (Abstracts for 1963): 221.

Rampton, V.

1038   1971 Late Quaternary Vegetational and Climatic History of the Snag-Klutlan Area, Southwestern Yukon Territory. Geological Society of America Bulletin 82: 959-978.

Ranere, A. J.
1039   1970 Prehistoric Environments and Cultural Continuity in the Western Great Basin. Tebiwa 13(2): 52-73.

1040   1971 Birch Creek Papers No. 4. Stratigraphy of Stone Tools from Meadow Canyon, Eastern Idaho. Occasional Papers of the Idaho State University Museum 27.

Raup, H. M.
1041   1937 Recent Changes of Climate and Vegetation in Southern New England and Adjacent New York. Journal of the Arnold Arboretum 18: 79-117.

1042   1938 Botanical Studies in the Black Rock Forest. Black Rock Forest Bulletin 7.

1043   1941 Botanical Problems in Boreal America. Botanical Review 7: 147-248.

1044   1947 The Botany of Southwestern Mackenzie. Sargentia 6.

Ray, L. L.
1045   1940 Glacial Chronology of the Southern Rocky Mountains. Geological Society of America Bulletin 51: 1851-1918.

Reed, E. K.
1046   1944 The Abandonment of the San Juan Region. El Palacio 51: 61-74.

Reeves, B. O. K.
1047   1969 The Southern Alberta Paleo-Cultural - Paleo-Environmental Sequence. In, R. G. Forbis, et. al. (eds.), Post-Pleistocene Man and His Environment on the Northern Plains. <u>Proceedings of the First Annual Paleo-Environmental Workshop of the University of Calgary Archaeological Association</u>, pp. 6-46. The Student's Press, University of Calgary, Calgary.

1048   1973 The Concept of an Altithermal Cultural Hiatus in Northern Plains Prehistory. <u>American Anthropologist</u> 75: 1221-1253.

Reeves, B. O. K., and J. F. Dormaar
1049   1972 A Partial Holocene Pedological and Archaeological Record from the Southern Alberta Rocky Mountains. <u>Arctic and Alpine Research</u> 4: 325-336.

Reid, H. F.
1050   1896 Glacier Bay and its Glaciers. <u>United States Geological Survey Annual Report</u> 16(1): 421-461.

Repenning, C. A., D. M. Hopkins, and M. Rubin
1051   1964 Tundra Rodents in a Late Pleistocene Fauna from the Tofty Placer District, Central Alaska. <u>Arctic</u> 17: 177-197.

Review of Palaeobotany and Palynology (eds.)
1052   1969 Bibliography of Palaeopalynology 1836-1966. <u>Review of Palaeobotany and Palynology</u> 8: 5-572.

Richard, P.
1053   1971 Two Pollen Diagrams from the Quebec City Area, Canada. <u>Pollen et Spores</u> 13: 524-559.

Richards, H. G.
1054   1936 Molluscs Associated with Early Man in the Southwest. American Naturalist 70: 369-371.

Richards, R. R.
1055   1938 A Pollen Profile of Otterbein Bog, Warren County, Indiana. Butler University Botanical Studies 4: 128-140.

Richardson, F. L. W., Jr.
1056   1937 Review of "The Relation of North American Prehistory to Post-Glacial Climatic Fluctuations" by R. G. Fisher. American Antiquity 2: 237-241.

Richmond, G. M.
1057   1948 Modification of Blackwelder's Sequence of Pleistocene Glaciation in the Wind River Mountains, Wyoming. Geological Society of America Bulletin 59: 1400-1401.

1058   1954 Modification of the Glacial Chronology of the San Juan Mountains, Colorado. Science 119: 614-615.

1059   1960 Glaciation of the East Slope of Rocky Mountain National Park, Colorado. Geological Society of America Bulletin 71: 1371-1382.

1060   1961 New Evidence of the Age of Lake Bonneville from the Moraines in Little Cottonwood Canyon, Utah. United States Geological Survey Professional Paper 424-D: 127-128.

1061   1962 Quaternary Stratigraphy of the La Sal Mountains, Utah. United States Geological Survey Professional Paper 324.

1062   1965 Glaciation of the Rocky Mountains. In, H. E. Wright, Jr., and D. G. Frey (eds.), The Quaternary of the United States, pp. 217-230. Princeton University Press, Princeton.

1063   1972 Appraisal of the Future Climate of the Holocene in the Rocky Mountains. Quaternary Research 2: 315-322.

Richmond, G. M., R. B. Morrison, and H. J. Bissell
1064   1952 Correlation of the Late Quaternary Deposits of the La Sal Mountains, Utah, and of Lakes Bonneville and Lahontan by Means of Interstadial Soils. Geological Society of America Bulletin 63: 1369.

Richmond, G. M., et. al.
1065   1965 The Cordilleran Ice Sheet of the Northern Rocky Mountains, and Related Quaternary History of the Columbia Plateau. In, H. E. Wright, Jr., and D. G. Frey (eds.), The Quaternary of the United States, pp. 231-242. Princeton University Press, Princeton.

Rickert, D. A., and J. C. F. Tedrow
1066   1967 Pedologic Investigations on some Aeolian Deposits of Northern Alaska. Soil Science 104: 250-262.

Rigg, G. B., and H. R. Gould
1067   1957 Age of Glacier Peak Eruption and Chronology of Post-Glacial Peat Deposits in Washington and Surrounding Areas. American Journal of Science 255: 341-363.

Rigg, G. B., and C. T. Richardson
1068   1934 The Development of Sphagnum Bogs in the San Juan Islands. American Journal of Botany 21: 610-622.

Ritcnie, J. C.
1069   1964 Contributions to the Holocene Paleoecology of Westcentral Canada. I. The Riding Mountain Area. Canadian Journal of Botany 42: 181-196.

1070   1966 Aspects of the Late Pleistocene History of the Canadian Flora. In, R. L. Taylor and R. A. Ludwig (eds.), The Evolution of Canada's Flora, pp. 68-80. The University of Toronto Press, Toronto.

1071   1967 Holocene Vegetation of the Northwestern Precincts of the Glacial Lake Agassiz Area. In, W. J. Mayer-Oakes (ed.), Life, Land and Water, pp. 217-229. University of Manitoba Press, Winnipeg.

1072   1969 Absolute Pollen Frequencies and Carbon-14 Age of a Section of Holocene Lake Sediment from the Riding Mountain Area of Manitoba. Canadian Journal of Botany 47: 1345-1349.

1073   1972 Pollen Analysis of Late-Quaternary Sediments from the Arctic Treeline of the Mackenzie River Delta Region, Northwest Territories, Canada. In, Y. Vasari, H. Hyvärinen, and S. Hicks (eds.), Climatic Changes in Arctic Areas during the Last Ten-Thousand Years. Acta Universitatis Ouluensis, Series A: Scientiae Rerum Naturalium 3, Geologica 1: 253-271. University of Oulu, Oulu.

Ritchie, J. C., and B. de Vries
1074   1964 Contributions to the Holocene Paleoecology of Westcentral Canada: A Late-Glacial Deposit from the Missouri Coteau. Canadian Journal of Botany 42: 677-692.

Ritchie, J. C., and F. K. Hare
1075   1971 Late Quaternary Vegetation and Climate near the Arctic Tree Line of Northwestern North America. Quaternary Research 1: 331-342.

Ritchie, J. C., and S. Lichti-Federovich
1076   1968 Holocene Pollen Assemblages from the Tiger Hills, Manitoba. Canadian Journal of Earth Sciences 5: 873-880.

Roberts, M. F.
1077   1970 Late Glacial and Postglacial Environments in Southeastern Wyoming. Palaeogeography, Palaeoclimatology, Palaeoecology 8: 5-17.

Roosma, A.
1078   1958 A Climatic Record from Searles Lake, California. Science 128: 716.

Rosendahl, C. O.
1079   1948 A Contribution to the Knowledge of the Pleistocene Flora of Minnesota. Ecology 29: 284-315.

Rowley, J. R.
1080   1957 A Preliminary Pollen Study from a Fossil Bison Site in St. Paul, Minnesota. Minnesota Academy of Sciences Proceedings 25: 40-50.

Ruhe, R. V.
1081   1969 Quaternary Landscapes in Iowa. Iowa State University Press, Ames.

1082   1970 Soils, Paleosols, and Environment. In, W. Dort, Jr., and J. K. Jones, Jr., (eds.), Pleistocene and Recent Environments of the Central Great Plains. Department of Geology, University of Kansas, Special Publication 3: 37-52.

1083   1974 Holocene Environments and Soil Geomorphology in Midwestern United States. Quaternary Research 4: 487-495.

Ruhe, R. V., and W. H. Scholtes
1084   1955 Radiocarbon Dates in Central Iowa. Journal of Geology 63: 82-92.

Ruhe, R. V., M. Rubin, and W. H. Scholtes
1085   1957 Late Pleistocene Radiocarbon Chronology in Iowa. American Journal of Science 255: 671-689.

Russell, I. C.
1086   1885 Geological History of Lake Lahontan, a Quaternary Lake of Northwestern Nevada. United States Geological Survey Monographs II.

1087   1889 Quaternary History of Mono Valley, California. United States Geological Survey Annual Report 8: 261-394.

Russell, R. J.
1088   1941 Climatic Change through the Ages. In, Climate and Man, pp. 67-97. Yearbook of Agriculture, United States Department of Agriculture, Washington.

Saarnisto, M.
1089   1974 The Deglaciation History of the Lake Superior Region and its Climatic Implications. Quaternary Research 4: 316-339.

Sadek-Kooros, H.
1090   1972 The Sediments and Fauna of Jaguar Cave: I - The Sediments. Tebiwa 15(1): 1-20.

Sampson, A. W.
1091   1938 Review of "Rainfall and Treegrowth in the Great Basin" by E. Antevs. Carnegie Institute of Washington Publication 469 and American Geographical Society of New York Publication 21, 1938. Journal of Forestry 36: 1249-1251.

Sanger, D., and R. G. MacKay
1092   1973 The Hirundo Archaeological Project - Preliminary Report. Man in the Northeast 6: 21-30.

Sayles, E. B.
1093   1965 Late Quaternary Climate Recorded by Cochise Culture. American Antiquity 30: 476-480.

Sayles, E. B., and E. Antevs
1094   1941 The Cochise Culture. Medallion Papers 29.

Schmidt, K. P.
1095   1938 Herpetological Evidence for the Post-Glacial Eastward Expansion of Steppe in North America. Ecology 19: 396-407.

Schoenwetter, J.
1096   1962 A Late Postglacial Chronology from the Central Mississippi Valley. Pollen et Spores 4: 376.

1097 1962 The Pollen Analysis of Eighteen Archaeological Sites in Arizona and New Mexico. In, P. S. Martin, et. al., Chapters in the Prehistory of Eastern Arizona, I. Chicago Natural History Museum, Fieldiana (Anthropology) 53: 168-209.

1098 1965 Utah W:5:50: Palynological Analysis. In, A. H. Schroeder, Salvage Excavations at Natural Bridges National Monument. University of Utah Anthropological Papers 10: 102-103.

1099 1966 A Re-Evaluation of the Navajo Reservoir Pollen Chronology. El Palacio 73: 19-26.

1100 1967 Pollen Survey of the Chuska Valley. In, A. H. Harris, J. Schoenwetter, and A. H. Warren, An Archaeological Survey of the Chuska Valley and Chaco Plateau, New Mexico. Part I: Natural Science Studies. Museum of New Mexico Research Records 4: 72-103.

1101 1970 Archaeological Pollen Studies of the Colorado Plateau. American Antiquity 35-48.

1102 1974 Pollen Analysis of Sediments from Salts Cave Vestibule. In, P. J. Watson (ed.), Archeology of the Mammoth Cave Area, pp. 97-105. Academic Press, New York.

Schoenwetter, J., and A. E. Dittert, Jr.
1103 1968 An Ecological Interpretation of Anasazi Settlement Patterns. In, B. J. Meggers (ed.), Anthropological Archaeology in the Americas, pp. 41-66. Anthropological Society of Washington, Washington.

Schoenwetter, J., and F. W. Eddy
1104   1964 Alluvial and Palynological Reconstruction of Environments, Navajo Reservoir District. <u>Museum of New Mexico Papers in Anthropology</u> 13.

Schofield, W. B., and H. Robinson
1105   1960 Late-Glacial and Postglacial Plant Macrofossils from Gillis Lake, Richmond County, Nova Scotia. <u>American Journal of Science</u> 258: 518-523.

Schove, D. J.
1106   1961 Tree Rings and Climatic Chronology. <u>New York Academy of Sciences Annals</u> 95: 605-622.

Schrock, A. E.
1107   1945 A Preliminary Analysis of an Unglaciated Bog in Pennsylvania. <u>University of Pittsburgh Bulletin</u> 41: 1-4.

Schulman, E.
1108   1938 Nineteen Centuries of Rainfall History in the Southwest. <u>American Meteorological Society Bulletin</u> 19: 211-215.

1109   1938 Review of "Rainfall and Tree Growth in the Great Basin" by Ernst Antevs. <u>American Meteorological Society Bulletin</u> 19: 216-217.

1110   1940 A Bibliography of Tree Ring Analysis. <u>Tree-Ring Bulletin</u> 6: 27-39.

1111   1941 Precipitation Records in California Treerings. <u>Sixth Pacific Science Congress Proceedings (1939)</u> 3: 707-717.

1112   1942 Dendrochronology in Pines of Arkansas. Ecology 23: 309-318.

1113   1945 Tree-Ring Hydrology of the Colorado River Basin. University of Arizona Bulletin 16(4); Laboratory of Tree-Ring Research Bulletin 2.

1114   1947 Tree-Ring Hydrology in Southern California. University of Arizona Bulletin 18(3); Laboratory of Tree-Ring Research Bulletin 4.

1115   1948 Dendrochronology at Navajo National Monument. Tree-Ring Bulletin 14: 18-24.

1116   1948 Dendrochronology in Northeastern Utah. Tree-Ring Bulletin 15: 2-14.

1117   1949 An Extension of the Durango Chronology. Tree-Ring Bulletin 16: 12-16.

1118   1949 Early Chronologies in the San Juan Basin. Tree-Ring Bulletin 15: 24-32.

1119   1950 Dendroclimatic Histories in the Bryce Canyon Area, Utah. Tree-Ring Bulletin 17: 2-16.

1120   1951 Tree-Ring Indices of Rainfall, Temperature, and River Flow. In, T. F. Malone (ed.), Compendium of Meteorology, pp. 1024-1029. American Meteorological Society, Boston.

1121   1952 Dendroclimatic Changes in Semiarid Regions. Tree-Ring Bulletin 20: 26-30.

1122   1952 Extension of the San Juan Chronology to B. C. Times. Tree-Ring Bulletin 18: 30-35.

1123   1953 Rio Grande Chronologies. Tree-Ring Bulletin 19: 20-33.

1124   1953 Tree-Ring Evidence for Climatic Change. In, H. Shaplow (ed.), Climatic Change, pp. 209-219. Harvard University Press, Cambridge.

1125   1954 Tree-Rings and History in the Western United States. Economic Botany 8: 234-250. (Reprinted in Smithsonian Institution Annual Report 1955: 459-473).

1126   1956 Dendroclimatic Changes in Semiarid America. University of Arizona Press, Tucson.

Schultz, C. B., and E. B. Howard
1127   1935 The Fauna of Burnet Cave, Guadalupe Mountains, New Mexico. Academy of Natural Sciences of Philadelphia Proceedings 87: 273-298.

Schultz, G. E.
1128   1967 Four Superimposed Late-Pleistocene Vertebrate Faunas from Southwest Kansas. In, P. S. Martin and H. E. Wright, Jr. (eds.), Pleistocene Extinctions, pp. 321-336. Yale University Press, New Haven.

1129   1969 Geology and Paleontology of a Late Pleistocene Basin in Southwest Kansas. Geological Society of America Special Paper 105.

Schumm, S. A., and R. F. Hadley
1130   1957 Arroyos and the Semi-Arid Cycle of Erosion. American Journal of Science 255: 161-174.

Schwartz, D. W.
1131   1957 Climate Change and Culture History in the Grand Canyon Region. American Antiquity 22: 372-377.

Schwarzbach, M.
1132   1963 Climates of the Past. Van Nostrand, London.

Schweger, C. E.
1133   1969 Pollen Analysis of Iola Bog and Paleoecology of the Two Creeks Forest Bed, Wisconsin. Ecology 50: 859-868.

Scott, G. R.
1134   1963 Quaternary Geology and Geomorphic History of the Kassler Quadrangle, Colorado. United States Geological Survey Professional Paper 421-A.

Sears, P. B.
1135   1926 The Natural Vegetation of Ohio. III. Plant Succession. Ohio Journal of Science 26: 213-231.

1136   1930 A Record of Post-Glacial Climate in Northern Ohio. Ohio Journal of Science 30: 205-217.

1137   1931 Pollen Analysis of Mud Bog Lake in Ohio. Ecology 12: 650-655.

1138   1931 Post-Glacial Climate in North America. Fifth International Botanical Congress, Report of Proceedings: 68.

1139   1931 Recent Climate and Vegetation a Factor in Mound Building Cultures? Science 73: 640-641.

1140   1932 Postglacial Climate in Eastern North America. Ecology 13: 1-6.

1141   1932 The Archaeology of Environment in Eastern North America. American Anthropologist 34: 610-622.

1142   1933 Climatic Change as a Factor in Forest Succession. Journal of Forestry 31: 934-942.

1143   1935 Glacial and Postglacial Vegetation. Botanical Review 1: 37-51.

1144   1935 Types of North American Pollen Profiles. Ecology 16: 488-499.

1145   1937 Pollen Analysis as an Aid to Dating Cultural Deposits in the United States. In, G. G. MacCurdy (ed.), Early Man, pp. 61-66. Lippincott, Philadelphia.

1146   1938 Climatic Interpretation of Postglacial Pollen Deposits in North America. American Meteorological Society Bulletin 19: 177-185.

1147   1941 A Submerged Migration Route. Science 94: 301.

1148   1941 Postglacial Vegetation in the Erie-Ohio Area. Ohio Journal of Science 41: 225-234.

1149   1942 Forest Sequences in the North Central States. Botanical Gazette 103: 751-761.

1150   1942 Postglacial Migration of Five Forest Genera. American Journal of Botany 29: 684-691.

1151   1942 Xerothermic Theory. Botanical Review 8: 708-736.

1152   1948 Forest Sequence and Climatic Change in Northeastern North America since Early Wisconsin Time. Ecology 29: 326-333.

1153   1950 Forest Sequence and Climatic Changes in Northeastern North America since Early Wisconsin Times. In, J. D. Jennings (ed.), Proceedings of the Sixth Plains Archaeological Conference. University of Utah Anthropological Papers II: 67-69.

1154   1951 Palynology in North America. Svensk Botanisk Tidskrift 45: 241-246.

1155   1954 Changes in Quaternary Climate and Vegetation Indicated by Pollen Analysis in North America. Eighth International Botanical Congress, Paris, Comptes Rendus, Section 6: 243-245.

1156   1958 Environment and Culture in Retrospect. In, T. L. Smiley (ed.), Climate and Man in the Southwest. University of Arizona Bulletin 28(4): 77-84.

1157   1961 A Pollen Profile from the Grassland Province. Science 134: 2038-2040.

1158   1961 Palynology and the Climatic Record of the Southwest. New York Academy of Sciences Annals 95: 632-641.

1159   1963 Vegetation, Climate, and Coastal Submergence in Connecticut. Science 140: 59-60.

Sears, P. B., and M. Bopp
1160 1960 Pollen Analysis of the Michillinda Peat Seam. Ohio Journal of Science 60: 149-154.

Sears, P. B., and K. H. Clisby
1161 1952 Pollen Spectra Associated with the Orleton Farms Mastodon Site. Ohio Journal of Science 52: 9-10.

1162 1952 Two Long Climatic Records. Science 116: 176-178.

Sears, P. B., and G. C. Couch
1163 1932 Microfossils in an Arkansas Peat and Their Significance. Ohio Journal of Science 32: 63-68.

Sears, P. B., and E. Jansen
1164 1933 The Rate of Peat Growth in the Erie Basin. Ecology 14: 348-355.

Sears, P. B., and A. Roosma
1165 1961 A Climatic Sequence from Two Nevada Caves. American Journal of Science 259: 669-678.

Sears, P. B., et. al.
1166 1955 Introduction and Acknowledgements. In, Palynology in Southern North America. Geological Society of America Bulletin 66: 471-473.

Semken, H. A.
1167 1969 Paleontological Implications of Micromammals from Peccary Cave, Newton County, Arkansas. Abstracts with Programs for 1969, Part 2: 27. Geological Society of America.

Semken, H. A., B. B. Miller, and J. B. Stevens
1168   1964 Late Wisconsin Woodland Musk Oxen in Association with Pollen and Invertebrates from Michigan. Journal of Paleontology 38: 823-835.

Senter, D.
1169   1937 Tree Rings, Valley Floor Deposition, and Erosion in Chaco Canyon, New Mexico. American Antiquity 3: 68-75.

Sharp, R. P.
1170   1951 Glacial History of Wolf Creek, St. Elias Range, Canada. Journal of Geology 59: 97-117.

1171   1958 The Latest Major Advance of Malaspina Glacier, Alaska. Geographical Review 48: 16-26.

1172   1960 Pleistocene Glaciation in the Trinity Alps of Northern California. American Journal of Science 258: 305-340.

Sharp, R. P., G. R. Allen, and M. F. Meier
1173   1959 Pleistocene Glaciers of Southern California Mountains. American Journal of Science 257: 81-94.

Shay, C. T.
1174   1967 Vegetation History of the Southern Lake Agassiz Basin during the Past 12,000 Years. In, W. J. Mayer-Oakes (ed.), Life, Land and Water, pp. 231-252. University of Manitoba Press, Winnipeg.

1175   1971 The Itasca Bison Kill Site· An Ecological Analysis. Minnesota Prehistoric Archaeology Series, Minnesota Historical Society, St. Paul.

Shutler, M. E., and R. E. Shutler, Jr.
1176   1963 Deer Creek Cave, Elko County, Nevada. Nevada State Museum Anthropological Papers 11.

Shutler, R. E., Jr.
1177   1961 Correlation of Beach Terraces with Climatic Cycles of Pluvial Lake Lahontan, Nevada. New York Academy of Sciences Annals 95: 513-520.

Shutler, R. E., Jr., et. al.
1178   1960 Stuart Rockshelter, A Stratified Site in Southern Nevada. Nevada State Museum Anthropological Papers 3.

Sigafoos, R. S., and E. L. Hendricks
1179   1961 Botanical Evidence of Glacier Activity at Mt. Rainier, Washington. Ecological Society of America Bulletin 42: 137.

1180   1961 Botanical Evidence of the Modern History of Nisqually Glacier, Washington. United States Geological Survey Professional Paper 387-A.

Sirkin, L. A.
1181   1965 Late-Pleistocene Pollen Stratigraphy of Western Long Island and Eastern Staten Island, New York. Adelphi University Science Journal 15.

1182   1967 Correlation of Late Glacial Pollen Stratigraphy and Environments in Northeastern U. S. A. Review of Palaeobotany and Palynology 2: 205-218.

1183   1967 Late-Pleistocene Pollen Stratigraphy of Western Long Island and Eastern Staten Island, New York. In, E. J. Cushing and H. E. Wright, Jr. (eds.), Quaternary Paleoecology, pp. 249-274. Yale University Press, New Haven.

1184   1971 Surficial Glacial Deposits and Postglacial Pollen Stratigraphy in Central Long Island, New York. Pollen et Spores 13: 93-100.

Skeels, M. A.
1185   1962 The Mastodons and Mammoths of Michigan. Michigan Academy of Science Papers 47: 101-133.

Slaughter, B. H.
1186   1966 The Vertebrates of the Domebo Local Fauna, Pleistocene of Oklahoma. In, F. Leonhardy (ed.), Domebo: A Paleo-Indian Mammoth Kill in the Prairie-Plains. Contributions of the Museum of the Great Plains 1: 31-35. Lawton.

1187   1967 Animal Ranges as a Clue to Late-Pleistocene Extinctions. In, P. S. Martin and H. E. Wright, Jr. (eds.), Pleistocene Extinctions, pp. 155-167. Yale University Press, New Haven.

Slaughter, B. H., and B. R. Hoover
1188   1963 Sulpher River Formation and the Pleistocene Mammals of the Ben Franklin Local Fauna. Southern Methodist University Graduate Research Center Journal 31: 132-148.

Smiley, T. L.
1189   1958 Years, Centuries, and Millenia. In, T. L. Smiley (ed.), Climate and Man in the Southwest. University of Arizona Bulletin 28(4): 11-18.

1190   1961 Evidences of Climatic Fluctuations in Southwestern Prehistory. <u>New York Academy of Sciences Annals</u> 95: 697-704.

Smiley, T. L., S. A. Stubbs, and B. Bannister
1191   1953 A Foundation for the Dating of some Late Archaeological Sites in the Rio Grande Area, New Mexico: Based on Studies in Tree-Ring Methods and Pottery Analyses. <u>University of Arizona Bulletin</u> 24(3); <u>Laboratory of Tree-Ring Research Bulletin</u> 6.

Smith, C. S.
1192   1950 Climate and Archaeology in Kansas. In, J. D. Jennings (ed.), Proceedings of the Sixth Plains Archaeological Conference. <u>University of Utah Anthropological Papers</u> II: 98-99.

Smith, G. I.
1193   1958 Late Quaternary Stratigraphy and Climatic Significance of Searles Lake, California. <u>Geological Society of America Bulletin</u> 69: 1706.

1194   1962 Subsurface Stratigraphy of Late Quaternary Deposits, Searles Lake, California: A Summary. <u>United States Geological Survey Professional Paper</u> 450-C: 65-69.

1195   1968 Late Quaternary Geologic and Climatic History of Searles Lake, Southeastern California. In, R. B. Morrison and H. E. Wright, Jr. (eds.), <u>Means of Correlation of Quaternary Successions</u>, pp. 293-310. University of Utah Press, Salt Lake City.

Smith, G. I., and D. V. Haines
1196   1964 Character and Distribution of Monoclastic Minerals in the Searles Lake Evaporite Deposit, California. United States Geological Survey Bulletin 1181-P.

Smith, H. T. U.
1197   1965 Dune Morphology and Chronology in Central and Western Nebraska. Journal of Geology 73: 557-578.

Smith, P.
1198   1940 Correlations of Pollen Profiles from Glaciated Eastern North America. American Journal of Science 238: 597-601.

Smith, P. W.
1199   1953 The Lined Snake in Illinois. Living Museum 15: 405-406.

1200   1957 An Analysis of Post-Wisconsin Biogeography of the Prairie Peninsula Based on Distributional Phenomena among Terrestrial Vertebrate Populations. Ecology 38: 205-218.

1201   1965 Recent Adjustments in Animal Ranges. In, H. E. Wright, Jr., and D. G. Frey (eds.), The Quaternary of the United States, pp. 633-642. Princeton University Press, Princeton.

Smith, P. W., and S. A. Minton, Jr.
1202   1957 A Distributional Summary of the Herpetofauna of Indiana and Illinois. American Midland Naturalist 58: 341-351.

Smith, P. W., and H. M. Smith
1203   1962 The Systematic and Biogeographic Status of Two Illinois Snakes. <u>C. C. Adams Center for Ecological Studies Occasional Papers 5</u>.

Smith, W. M.
1204   1937 Pollen Spectrum of Lake Cicott Bog, Cass County, Indiana. <u>Butler University Botanical Studies</u> 4: 43-54.

Sollberger, J. B., and T. R. Hester
1205   1972 The Strohacker Site: A Review of Pre-Archaic Manifestations in Texas. <u>Plains Anthropologist</u> 17: 326-344.

Sorenson, C. J., et. al.
1206   1971 Paleosols and the Forest Border in Keewatin, N. W. T. <u>Quaternary Research</u> 1: 468-473.

Spurr, S. H.
1207   1953 The Vegetational Significance of Recent Temperature Changes along the Atlantic Seaboard. <u>American Journal of Science</u> 251: 682-688.

Spurr, S. H., and J. E. Zumberge
1208   1956 Late Pleistocene Features of Cheboygan and Emmet Counties, Michigan. <u>American Journal of Science</u> 254: 96-109.

Stearns, C. E.
1209   1942 A Fossil Marmot from New Mexico and its Climatic Significance. <u>American Journal of Science</u> 240: 867-878.

Stein, W. T.
1210 1963 Mammal Remains from Archaeological Sites in the Point of Pines Region, Arizona. <u>American Antiquity</u> 29: 213-220.

Stingelin, R. W.
1211 1966 Late-Glacial and Post-Glacial Vegetational History in the North Central Appalachian Region. <u>Dissertation Abstracts</u> 26: 6650.

Stokes, M. A., and T. L. Smiley
1212 1963 Tree-Ring Dates from the Navajo Land Claim. I. The Northern Sector. <u>Tree-Ring Bulletin</u> 25: 8-18.

1213 1964 Tree-Ring Dates from the Navajo Land Claim. II. The Western Sector. <u>Tree-Ring Bulletin</u> 26: 13-27.

1214 1966 Tree-Ring Dates from the Navajo Land Claim. III. The Southern Sector. <u>Tree-Ring Bulletin</u> 27: 2-11.

1215 1969 Tree-Ring Dates from the Navajo Land Claim. IV. The Eastern Sector. <u>Tree-Ring Bulletin</u> 29: 2-14.

Stoutamire, W. F., and W. S. Benninghoff
1216 1964 Biotic Assemblage Associated with a Mastodon Skull from Oakland County, Michigan. <u>Papers of the Michigan Academy of Sciences, Arts and Letters</u> 49: 47-60.

Strong, W. D.
1217 1935 An Introduction to Nebraska Archaeology. <u>Smithsonian Miscellaneous Collections</u> 93(10).

Stuiver, M.
1218   1964 Carbon Isotopic Distribution and Correlated Chronology of Searles Lake Sediments. American Journal of Science 262: 377-392.

Stuiver, M., E. S. Deevey, Jr., and J. L. Gralenski
1219   1960 Yale Radiocarbon Measurements V. American Journal of Science Radiocarbon Supplement 2: 49-61.

Suess, H. E.
1220   1968 Climatic Changes, Solar Activity, and the Cosmic Ray Production Rates of the Natural Radiocarbon. Meteorological Monographs 8: 146-150.

1221   1971 Climatic Changes and the Atmospheric Radiocarbon Level. Palaeogeography, Palaeoclimatology, Palaeoecology 10: 199-202.

Swain, A. M.
1222   1973 A History of Fire and Vegetation in Northeastern Minnesota as Recorded in Lake Sediments. Quaternary Research 3: 383-396.

Swain, F. M.
1223   1965 Geochemistry of some Quaternary Lake Sediments of North America. In, H. E. Wright, Jr., and D. G. Frey (eds.), The Quaternary of the United States, pp. 765-781. Princeton University Press, Princeton.

Swanson, E. H., Jr.
1224   1961 Preliminary Report on Archaeology in the Birch Creek Valley, Eastern Idaho. Tebiwa 4(1): 25-28.

| 1225 | 1962 Early Cultures in Northwestern America. *American Antiquity* 28: 151-158. |

| 1226 | 1962 The Emergence of Plateau Culture. *Occasional Papers of the Idaho State University Museum* 8. |

| 1227 | 1964 Geochronology of the DjRi3 Site, British Columbia, 1959. *Tebiwa* 7(2): 42-52. |

| 1228 | 1966 The Geographic Foundations of the Desert Culture. In, W. d'Azevedo, et. al. (eds.), The Current Status of Anthropological Research in the Great Basin: 1964. *Desert Research Institute Social Sciences and Humanities Publications* 1: 137-146. University of Nevada, Reno. |

| 1229 | 1967-1968 Prehistoric Environments in Southeastern Idaho. *Idaho Yesterdays* 11(4): 20-22. |

| 1230 | 1969 Radiocarbon Dates for a Soil in Eastern Idaho. *Tebiwa* 12(2): 58-61. |

| 1231 | 1972 *Birch Creek: Human Ecology in the Cool Desert of the Northern Rocky Mountains 9000 B. C. - A. D. 1850.* Idaho State University Press, Pocatello. |

Swanson, E. H., Jr., and A. L. Bryan
| 1232 | 1964 Birch Creek Papers No. 1. An Archaeological Reconnaissance in the Birch Creek Valley of Eastern Idaho. *Occasional Papers of the Idaho State University Museum* 13. |

Swanson, E. H., Jr., and J. Dayley
| 1233 | 1968 Hunting at Malad Hill in Southeastern Idaho. *Tebiwa* 11(2): 59-69. |

Swanson, E. H., Jr., B. R. Butler, and R. Bonnichsen
1234   1964 Birch Creek Papers No. 2. Natural and Cultural Stratigraphy in the Birch Creek Valley of Eastern Idaho. <u>Occasional Papers of the Idaho State University Museum</u> 14.

Swickard, D. A.
1235   1941 Comparison of Pollen Spectra from Bogs of Early and Late Wisconsin Glaciation in Indiana. <u>Butler University Botanical Studies</u> 5: 67-84.

Tedrow, J. C. F.
1236   1972 Soil Morphology as an Indicator of Climatic Changes in the Arctic Areas. In, Y. Vasari, H. Hyvärinen, and S. Hicks (eds.), Climatic Changes in Arctic Areas during the Last Ten-Thousand Years. <u>Acta Universitatis Ouluensis, Series A: Scientiae Rerum Naturalium 3, Geologica</u> I: 61-74. University of Oulu, Oulu.

Tedrow, J. C. F., and G. F. Walton
1237   1964 Some Quaternary Events of Northern Alaska. <u>Arctic</u> 17: 286-271.

Terasmae, J.
1238   1959 Notes on the Champlain Sea Episode in the St. Lawrence Lowland, Quebec. <u>Science</u> 130: 334-336.

1239   1960 A Palynological Study of Post-Glacial Deposits in the St. Lawrence Lowlands. <u>Geological Survey of Canada Bulletin</u> 56: 1-22.

1240   1961 Notes on Late-Quaternary Climatic Changes in Canada. <u>New York Academy of Sciences Annals</u> 95: 658-675.

1241   1963 Problems of Pollen Zone Correlation in Southeastern Canada. Grana Palynologica 4: 313-318.

1242   1963 Three C-14 Dated Pollen Profiles from Newfoundland, Canada. Advancing Frontiers of Plant Sciences 6: 149-162.

1243   1965 Postglacial Chronology and Forest History in the Northern Lake Huron and Superior Region. International Association for Quaternary Research, Seventh Congress, General Sessions Abstracts: 463.

1244   1965 Problems of Quaternary Palynology in the Canadian Arctic. International Association for Quaternary Research, Seventh Congress, General Sessions Abstracts: 464-465.

1245   1967 A Review of Quaternary Paleobotany and Palynology in Canada. Geological Survey of Canada Papers 67-13.

1246   1967 Postglacial Chronology and Forest History in the Northern Lake Huron and Lake Superior Regions. In, E. J. Cushing and H. E. Wright, Jr. (eds.), Quaternary Paleoecology, pp. 45-48. Yale University Press, New Haven.

1247   1967 Recent Pollen Deposition in the Northeastern District of Mackenzie (Northwest Territories, Canada). Palaeogeography, Palaeoclimatology, Palaeoecology 3: 17-27.

1248   1968 A Discussion of Deglaciation and the Boreal Forest History in the Northern Great Lakes Region. Entomological Society of Ontario Proceedings 99: 31-43.

1249   1968 Late Quaternary Geochronology and Deglaciation in Northwestern Canada. In, A. H. Stryd and R. A. Smith (eds.), Aboriginal Man and Environments on the Plateau of Northwest America, pp. 243-252. The Student's Press, University of Calgary, Calgary.

1250   1968 Some Problems of the Quaternary Palynology in the Western Mainland Region of the Canadian Arctic. Geological Survey of Canada Papers 68-23.

1251   1969 Quaternary Palynology in Quebec: A Review and Future Prospects. Revue de Géographie de Montréal 13(3): 281-288.

1252   1972 The Pleistocene-Holocene Boundary in the Canadian Context. Twenty Fourth International Geological Congress, Section 12: 120-125.

1253   1973 Notes on Late Wisconsin and Early Holocene History of Vegetation in Canada. Arctic and Alpine Research 5: 201-222.

Terasmae, J., and T. W. Anderson
1254   1970 Hypsithermal Range Extension of White Pine (Pinus strobus L.) in Quebec, Canada. Canadian Journal of Earth Sciences 7: 406-413.

Terasmae, J., and B. G. Craig
1255   1958 Discovery of Fossil Ceratophyllum demersum L. in Northwest Territories, Canada. Canadian Journal of Botany 36: 567-569.

Terasmae, J., and J. G. Fyles
1256   1959 Paleobotanical Studies of Late-Glacial Deposits from Vancouver Island, British Columbia. Canadian Journal of Botany 37: 815-817.

Terasmae, J., and O. L. Hughes
1257 1960 A Palynological and Geological Study of Pleistocene Deposits in the James Bay Lowlands, Ontario. Geological Survey of Canada Bulletin 62.

1258 1966 Late Wisconsinan Chronology and History of Vegetation in the Ogilvie Mountains, Yukon Territory, Canada. Paleobotanist 15: 235-242.

Terasmae, J., and P. Lasalle
1259 1968 Notes on Late-Glacial Palynology and Geochronology at St. Hilaire, Quebec. Canadian Journal of Earth Sciences 5: 249-257.

Terasmae, J., and R. J. Mott
1260 1971 Postglacial History and Palynology of Sable Island, Nova Scotia. Geoscience and Man 3: 17-28.

Terasmae, J., P. Webber, and J. Andrews
1261 1966 A Study of Late Quaternary Plant-Bearing Beds in North-Central Baffin Island, Canada. Arctic 19: 296-318.

Thomas, E. S.
1262 1951 Distribution of Ohio Animals. Ohio Journal of Science 51: 153-167.

1263 1952 The Orleton Farms Mastodon. Ohio Journal of Science 52: 1-5.

Thomas, H. E.
1264 1962 The Meteorologic Phenomenon of Drought in the Southwest. United States Geological Survey Paper 372-A.

Thomas, M. K.
1265   1957 Changes in the Climate of Ontario. In, F. A. Urquhart (ed.), Changes in the Fauna of Ontario, pp. 59-75. University of Toronto Press, Toronto.

Transeau, E. N.
1266   1935 The Prairie Peninsula. Ecology 16: 423-437.

1267   1941 Prehistoric Factors in the Development of the Vegetation of Ohio. Ohio Journal of Science 41: 207-211.

Trewartha, G. T.
1268   1940 The Vegetal Cover of the Driftless Cuestaform Hill Land: Pre-Settlement Record and Postglacial Evolution. Transactions of the Wisconsin Academy of Sciences, Arts and Letters 32: 361-382.

Truman, H. V.
1269   1937 Fossil Evidence of Two Prairie Invasions of Wisconsin. Transactions of the Wisconsin Academy of Sciences, Arts and Letters 30: 36-42.

Tucker, J. M., W. P. Cottam, and R. Drobnick
1270   1961 Studies on the Quercus undulata Complex. II. The Contribution of Quercus turbinella. American Journal of Botany 48: 329-339.

Tuohy, D., and E. H. Swanson, Jr.
1271   1960 Excavations at Rockshelter 10-AA-15, Southwest Idaho. Tebiwa 3(1/2): 20-24.

Upson, J. E., E. B. Leopold, and M. Rubin
1272   1964 Postglacial Change of Level in New Haven Harbor, Connecticut. American Journal of Science 262: 121-132.

Uyeno, T.
1273   1963 Late Pleistocene Fishes of the Clear Creek and Ben Franklin Local Faunas of Texas. Southern Methodist University Graduate Research Center Journal 31: 168-173.

Vallentyne, J. R., and Y. S. Swabey
1274   1955 A Reinvestigation of the History of Lower Linsley Pond, Connecticut. American Journal of Science 253: 313-340.

Van Royen, W.
1275   1936 The Problem of Postglacial Climate. American Meteorological Society Bulletin 17: 246-251.

1276   1937 Prehistoric Droughts in the Central Great Plains. Geographical Review 27: 637-650.

Van Stone, J. W.
1277   1953 Notes on Kotzebue Dating. Tree-Ring Bulletin 20: 6-8.

Van Winkle, W.
1278   1914 Quality of the Surface Waters of Oregon. United States Geological Survey Water-Supply Paper 363.

Vasari, Y., H. Hyvärinen, and S. Hicks (eds.)
1279   1972 Climatic Changes in Arctic Areas during the Last Ten-Thousand Years. Acta Universitatis Ouluensis Series A: Scientiae Rerum Naturalium 3, Geologica 1. University of Oulu, Oulu.

Vaufrey, R.
1280   1946 L'Analyse des Pollens en Amérique. L'Anthropologie 50: 299-300.

Viereck, L. A.
1281   1968 Botanical Dating of Recent Glacial Activity in Western North America. In, H. E. Wright, Jr., and W. H. Osburn (eds.), Arctic and Alpine Environments, pp. 189-204. Indiana University Press, Bloomington.

Voss, J.
1282   1931 Preliminary Report on the Paleoecology of a Wisconsin and an Illinois Bog. Illinois Academy of Science Transactions 24: 130-137.

1283   1934 A Stratigraphical Study of the Manito Swamp. Illinois Academy of Science Transactions 27: 66-68.

1284   1934 Postglacial Migration of Forests in Illinois, Wisconsin, and Minnesota. Botanical Gazette 96: 3-43.

1285   1937 Comparative Study of Bogs on Cary and Tazewell Drift in Illinois. Ecology 18: 119-135.

Waddington, J. C. B.
1286   1969 A Stratigraphic Record of the Pollen Influx to a Lake in the Big Woods of Minnesota. Geological Society of America Special Paper 123: 263-282.

Waddington, J. C. B., and H. E. Wright, Jr.
1287   1970 Late-Quaternary Vegetational Changes on the East Side of Yellowstone Park, Wyoming. American Quaternary Association, First Meeting, Abstracts: 139-140.

1288 1974 Late Quaternary Vegetational Changes on the East Side of Yellowstone Park, Wyoming. Quaternary Research 4: 175-184.

Wahraftig, C., and J. H. Birman
1289 1965 The Quaternary of the Pacific Mountain System in California. In, H. E. Wright, Jr., and D. G. Frey (eds.), The Quaternary of the United States, pp. 299-340. Princeton University Press, Princeton.

Walker, P. C., and R. T. Hartman
1290 1960 The Forest Sequence of the Hartstown Bog Area in Western Pennsylvania. Ecology 41: 461-474.

Walker, P. H.
1291 1966 Postglacial Environments in Relation to Landscape and Soils on the Cary Drift, Iowa. Iowa State University Agriculture and Home Economics Experimental Station, Research Bulletin 549: 837-875.

1292 1966 Postglacial Erosion and Environment Changes in Central Iowa. Journal of Soil and Water Conservation 21: 21-23.

Walker, P. H., and G. S. Brush
1293 1964 Observations on Bog and Pollen Stratigraphy of the Des Moines Glacial Lobe. Iowa Academy of Science Proceedings 70: 253-260.

Ward, W. H.
1294 1952 The Glaciological Studies of the Baffin Island Expedition 1950: Part 2 - The Physics of Deglaciation of Central Baffin Island, with appendix by M. E. Hale. Journal of Glaciology 2: 9-23.

Warren, C. N.
1295   1968 The View from Wenas: A Study in Plateau Prehistory. Occasional Papers of the Idaho State University Museum 24.

Wasylikowa, K., and H. E. Wright, Jr.
1296   1970 Late-Glacial Plant Succession on an Abandoned Drainageway, Northeastern Minnesota. Acta Palaeobotanica II: 23-43.

Watson, P. J.
1297   1974 Prehistoric Horticulturalists. In, P. J. Watson (ed.), The Archeology of the Mammoth Cave Area, pp. 233-238. Academic Press, New York.

Watts, W. A.
1298   1967 Late-Glacial Plant Macrofossils from Minnesota. In, E. J. Cushing and H. E. Wright, Jr. (eds.), Quaternary Paleoecology, pp. 89-97. Yale University Press, New Haven.

1299   1969 A Pollen Diagram from Mud Lake, Marion County, North-Central Florida. Geological Society of America Bulletin 80: 631-642.

1300   1971 Postglacial and Interglacial Vegetation History of Southern Georgia and Central Florida. Ecology 52: 676-690.

Watts, W. A., and R. C. Bright
1301   1968 Pollen, Seed, and Mollusk Analysis of a Sediment Core from Pickerel Lake, Day County, South Dakota. Geological Society of America Bulletin 79: 855-876.

Watts, W. A., and T. C. Winter
1302   1966 Plant Macrofossils from Kirchner Marsh, Minnesota - A Paleoecological Study. Geological Society of America Bulletin 77: 1339-1360.

Watts, W. A., and H. E. Wright, Jr.
1303   1966 Late-Wisconsin Pollen and Seed Analysis from the Nebraska Sandhills. Ecology 47: 202-210.

Weakly, H. E.
1304   1943 A Tree-Ring Record of Precipitation in Western Nebraska. Journal of Forestry 41: 816-819.

1305   1950 Dendrochronology and Its Climatic Implications in the Central Plains. In, J. D. Jennings (ed.), Proceedings of the Sixth Plains Archaeological Conference. University of Utah Anthropological Papers 11: 90-94.

Webb, R. A., A. Johnston, and J. D. Soper
1306   1967 The Prairie World. In, W. G. Hardy (ed.), Alberta: A Natural History, pp. 93-115. M. G. Hurtig, Edmonton.

Webb, T., III
1307   1970 A Comparison of Climatic Change during the Postglacial between Wisconsin and East-Central Minnesota. Abstracts with Programs 2(7): 717. Geological Society of America.

Webb, T., III, and R. A. Bryson
1308   1972 Late- and Postglacial Climatic Change in the Northern Midwest, U. S. A.: Quantitative Estimates Derived from Fossil Pollen Spectra by Multivariate Statistical Analysis. Quaternary Research 2: 70-115.

Weber, R. H.
1309   1973 Geology of Mockingbird Gap Site in Central New Mexico. Abstracts with Programs 5(7): 857-858. Geological Society of America.

Weber, W. A.
1310   1965 Plant Geography in the Southern Rocky Mountains. In, H. E. Wright, Jr., and D. G. Frey (eds.), The Quaternary of the United States, pp. 453-467. Princeton University Press, Princeton.

Wedel, W. R.
1311   1941 Environment and Native Subsistence Economies in the Central Great Plains. Smithsonian Miscellaneous Collections 101(3).

1312   1950 Climate and Culture: Some Questions. In, J. D. Jennings (ed.), Proceedings of the Sixth Plains Archaeological Conference. University of Utah Anthropological Papers 11: 85-87.

1313   1953 Some Aspects of Human Ecology in the Great Plains. American Anthropologist 55: 499-514.

1314   1957 The Central North American Grassland: Man-Made or Natural. In, Studies in Human Ecology, pp. 39-69. Anthropological Society of Washington, Washington.

1315   1959 An Introduction to Kansas Archaeology. Bureau of American Ethnology Bulletin 174.

1316   1961 Prehistoric Man on the Great Plains. University of Oklahoma Press, Norman.

1317 1970 Some Environmental and Historical Factors of the Great Bend Aspect. In, W. Dort, Jr., and J. K. Jones, Jr., (eds.), Pleistocene and Recent Environments of the Central Great Plains. Department of Geology, University of Kansas, Special Publication 3: 131-140.

Wedel, W. R., and M. F. Kivett
1318 1956 Additional Data on the Woodruff Ossuary, Kansas. American Antiquity 21: 414-415.

Wedel, W. R., W. M. Husted, and J. H. Moss
1319 1968 Mummy Cave: Prehistoric Record from Rocky Mountains of Wyoming. Science 160: 184-186.

Wells, B. W., and S. G. Boyce
1320 1953 Carolina Bays: Additional Data on Their Origin, Age, and History. Journal of the Elisha Mitchell Scientific Society 69: 119-141.

Wells, P. V.
1321 1964 Pleistocene Vegetation in Mohave Desert: Some Woodrat Midden Evidence. Ecological Society of America Bulletin 45: 76.

1322 1965 Scarp Woodlands, Transported Grassland Soils, and Concepts of Grassland Climate in the Great Plains Region. Science 148: 246-249.

1323 1966 Late Pleistocene Vegetation and Degree of Pluvial Climatic Change in the Chihuahuan Desert. Science 153: 970-975.

1324 1970 Postglacial Vegetational History of the Great Plains. Science 167: 1574-1582.

1325   1970 Vegetational History of the Great Plains: A Post-Glacial Record of Coniferous Woodland in Southeastern Wyoming. In, W. Dort, Jr., and J. K. Jones, Jr. (eds.), Pleistocene and Recent Environments of the Central Great Plains. Department of Geology, University of Kansas, Special Publication 3: 185-202.

Wells, P. V., and R. Berger
1326   1967 Late Pleistocene History of Coniferous Woodland in the Mohave Desert. Science 155: 1640-1647.

Wells, P. V., and C. D. Jorgensen
1327   1964 Pleistocene Wood Rat Middens and Climatic Change in Mohave Desert - A Record of Juniper Woodlands. Science 143: 1171-1174.

Wendland, W. M., and R. A. Bryson
1328   1974 Dating Climatic Episodes of the Holocene. Quaternary Research 4: 9-24.

Wendorf, F.
1329   1961 A General Introduction to the Ecology of the Llano Estacado. In, F. Wendorf (ed.), Paleoecology of the Llano Estacado. Fort Burgwin Research Center Publications 1: 12-22. Museum of New Mexico Press, Sante Fe.

1330   1961 An Interpretation of Late Pleistocene Environments of the Llano Estacado. In, F. Wendorf (ed.), Paleoecology of the Llano Estacado. Fort Burgwin Research Center Publications 1: 115-133. Museum of New Mexico Press, Sante Fe.

1331   1970 The Lubbock Subpluvial. In, W. Dort, Jr., and J. K. Jones, Jr. (eds.), Pleistocene and Recent Environments of the Central Great Plains. Department of Geology, University of Kansas, Special Publication 3: 23-35.

Wendorf, F. (ed.)
1332   1961 Paleoecology of the Llano Estacado. Fort Burgwin Research Center Publications 1. Museum of New Mexico Press, Sante Fe.

Wendorf, F., and J. J. Hester
1333   1962 Early Man's Utilization of the Great Plains Environment. American Antiquity 28: 159-171.

Wendorf, F., and A. D. Krieger
1334   1959 New Light on the Midland Discovery. American Antiquity 25: 66-78.

Wendorf, F., et. al.
1335   1955 The Midland Discovery. University of Texas Press, Austin.

Wenner, C. G.
1336   1947 Pollen Diagrams from Labrador. Geografiska Annaler 29: 137-173.

Wentworth, C. K., and L. L. Ray
1337   1936 Studies of Certain Alaska Glaciers in 1931. Geological Society of America Bulletin 47: 879-934.

West, R.
1338   1955 The Recent History of the Commander Glacier. Canadian Alpine Journal 38: 99-101.

West, R. G.
1339   1961 Late- and Postglacial Vegetational History in Wisconsin, Particularly Changes Associated with the Valders Readvance. American Journal of Science 259: 766-783.

Wettlaufer, B., and W. J. Mayer-Oakes, et. al.
1340   1960 The Long Creek Site. Saskatchewan Museum of Natural History, Anthropological Series 2.

Wheeler, J. O.
1341   1961 Whitehorse Map-Area, Yukon Territory. 105D. Geological Survey of Canada Memoir 312.

Whitaker, R. H.
1342   1956 Vegetation of the Great Smoky Mountains. Ecological Monographs 26: 1-80.

Whitehead, D. R.
1343   1959 Fossil Pollen and Spores from the LoDaiska Site, Colorado. Denver Museum of Natural History Proceedings 8: 114-118.

1344   1964 Fossil Pine Pollen and Full-Glacial Vegetation in Southeastern North Carolina. Ecology 45: 767-777.

1345   1965 Palynology and Pleistocene Phytogeography of Unglaciated Eastern North America. In, H. E. Wright, Jr., and D. G. Frey (eds.), The Quaternary of the United States, pp. 417-432. Princeton University Press, Princeton.

1346   1967 Studies of Full-Glacial Vegetation and Climate in Southeastern United States. In, E. J. Cushing and H. E. Wright, Jr. (eds.), Quaternary Paleoecology, pp. 237-248. Yale University Press, New Haven.

1347   1972 Developmental and Environmental History of the Dismal Swamp. Ecological Monographs 42: 301-315.

1348   1973 Late-Wisconsin Vegetational Changes in Unglaciated Eastern North America. Quaternary Research 3: 621-631.

Whitehead, D. R., and D. R. Bentley
1349   1963 A Postglacial Pollen Diagram from Southwestern Vermont. Pollen et Spores 5: 115-127.

Whiteside, M. C.
1350   1965 Paleoecological Studies of Potato Lake and its Environs. Ecology 46: 807-816.

Will, G. F.
1351   1946 Tree Ring Studies in North Dakota. North Dakota Agricultural College, Agricultural Experimental Station Bulletin 338.

1352   1950 Dendrochronology, Climate, and Prehistory on the Upper Missouri. In, J. D. Jennings (ed.), Proceedings of the Sixth Plains Archaeological Conference. University of Utah Anthropological Papers 11: 95-97.

Willett, H. C.
1353   1949 Long-Period Fluctuations of the General Circulation of the Atmosphere. Journal of Meteorology 6: 34-50.

Williams, J. R., and O. J. Ferrians, Jr.
1354   1961 Late Wisconsin and Recent History of the Matanuska Glacier, Alaska. Arctic 14: 89-90.

Williams, J. S.
1355 1956 Geomorphic Effects of the Altithermal in Northern Utah. <u>Proceedings of the Utah Academy of Sciences, Arts and Letters</u> 33: 13-25.

Wilmeth, R. W.
1356 1970 Review of "The Northwestern Plains: A Symposium", ed. by W. W. Caldwell. <u>American Antiquity</u> 35: 116-117.

Wilson, I. T., and J. E. Potzger
1357 1943 Pollen Records from Lakes in Anoka County, Minnesota: A Study of Methods of Sampling. <u>Ecology</u> 24: 382-392.

1358 1943 Pollen Study of Sediments from Douglas Lake, Cheboygan County, and Middle Fish Lake, Montmorency County, Michigan. <u>Indiana Academy of Science Proceedings</u> 52: 87-92.

Wilson, L. R.
1359 1931 Evidence of a Lower Level of Lake Superior. <u>Science</u> 73: 185.

1360 1932 The Two Creeks Forest Bed, Manitowoc County, Wisconsin. <u>Transactions of the Wisconsin Academy of Sciences, Arts and Letters</u> 27: 31-46.

1361 1936 Further Fossil Studies of the Two Creeks Forest Bed, Manitowoc County, Wisconsin. <u>Bulletin of the Torrey Botanical Club</u> 63: 317-325.

1362 1938 The Postglacial History of Vegetation in Northwestern Wisconsin. <u>Rhodora</u> 40: 137-175.

1363   1938 The Use of Microfossils as a Means of Studying Paleoclimatic Conditions in Northwestern Wisconsin. American Meteorological Society Bulletin 19: 186.

1364   1944 "Fossil Evidence of Wider Post-Pleistocene Range for Butternut and Hickory in Wisconsin" - A Reply. Rhodora 46: 149-155.

1365   1949 A Microfossil Analysis of the Lower Peat and Associated Sediments at the John Hancock Fishweir Site. In, F. Johnson (ed.), The Boylston Street Fishweir II. Papers of the R. S. Peabody Foundation for Archaeology 4(1): 84-98.

1366   1966 Palynology of the Domebo Site. In, F. Leonhardy (ed.), Domebo: A Paleo-Indian Mammoth Kill in the Prairie-Plains. Contributions of the Museum of the Great Plains 1: 44-50. Lawton.

Wilson, L. R., and A. T. Cross
1367   1943 A Study of the Plant Micro-Fossil Succession in the Bottom Deposits of Crystal Lake, Vilas County, Wisconsin, and the Peat of an Adjacent Bog. American Journal of Science 241: 307-315.

Wilson, L. R., and E. F. Galloway
1368   1937 Microfossil Succession in a Bog in Northern Wisconsin. Ecology 18: 113-118.

Wilson, L. R., and R. M. Webster
1369   1942 Fossil Evidence and Wider Post-Pleistocene Range of Butternut and Hickory in Wisconsin. Rhodora 44: 409-414.

1370   1942 Microfossil Studies of Three North-Central Wisconsin Bogs. Transactions of the Wisconsin Academy of Sciences, Arts and Letters 34: 177-193.

Wilson, R. W.
1371   1942 Preliminary Study of the Fauna of Rampart Cave, Arizona. Carnegie Institute of Washington Publication 520: 169-185.

Winter, T. C.
1372   1962 Pollen Sequence at Kirchner Marsh, Minnesota. Science 138: 526-528.

Witt, A., Jr.
1373   1960 Length and Weight of Ancient Freshwater Drum, Aplodinotus grunniens, Calculated from Otoliths Found in Indian Middens. Copeia 3: 181-185.

Woodbury, R. B.
1374   1961 Climatic Changes and Prehistoric Agriculture in the Southwestern United States. New York Academy of Sciences Annals 95: 705-709.

Wormington, H. M., and D. Ellis (eds.)
1375   1967 Pleistocene Studies in Southern Nevada. Nevada State Museum Anthropological Papers 13.

Wormington, H. M., and R. G. Forbis
1376   1965 An Introduction to the Archaeology of Alberta, Canada. Denver Museum of Natural History Proceedings 11.

Wright, H. E., Jr.
1377   1964 Aspects of the Early Postglacial Forest Succession in the Great Lakes Region. Ecology 45: 439-448.

1378   1965 Late Glacial Vegetation History of the Lake Superior Region. University of Michigan Great Lakes Research Division Publication 13: 248.

1379   1966 Stratigraphy of Lake Sediments and the Precision of the Paleoclimatic Record. In, J. S. Sawyer (ed.), Proceedings of the International Symposium on World Climates 8000 to 0 B. C., pp. 157-173. Royal Meteorological Society, London.

1380   1968 History of the Prairie Peninsula. In, R. E. Bergstrom (ed.), The Quaternary of Illinois. University of Illinois College of Agriculture Special Publication 14: 78-88.

1381   1968 The Role of Pine and Spruce in the Forest History of Minnesota and Adjacent Areas. Ecology 49: 937-955.

1382   1969 Glacial Fluctuations and the Forest Succession in the Lake Superior Area. International Association for Great Lakes Research, Twelfth Conference Proceedings: 397-405.

1383   1970 Vegetational History of the Central Plains. In, W. Dort, Jr., and J. K. Jones, Jr. (eds.), Pleistocene and Recent Environments of the Central Great Plains. Department of Geology, University of Kansas, Special Publication 3: 157-172.

1384   1971 Late Quaternary Vegetational History of North America. In, K. K. Turekian (ed.), Late Cenozoic Glacial Ages, pp. 425-464. Yale University Press, New Haven.

1385   1971 Retreat of the Laurentide Ice Sheet from 14,000 to 9,000 Years Ago. Quaternary Research 1: 316-330.

1386   1972 Interglacial and Postglacial Climates: The Pollen Record. Quaternary Research 2: 274-282.

1387   1973 Tunnel Valleys, Glacial Surges, and Subglacial Hydrology of the Superior Lobe, Minnesota. In, R. F. Black, R. P. Goldthwait, and H. B. Willman (eds.), The Wisconsinan Stage. Geological Society of America Memoir 136: 251-276.

Wright, H. E., Jr., and D. G. Frey (eds.)
1388   1965 The Quaternary of the United States. Princeton University Press, Princeton.

Wright, H. E., Jr., and M. Rubin
1389   1956 Radiocarbon Dates of Mankato Drift in Minnesota. Science 124: 625-626.

Wright, H. E., Jr., and R. V. Ruhe
1390   1963 Retrospect on the Contributions of Geological Studies to Problems of the Climate of the Eleventh and Sixteenth Centuries - A Conservative View. In, R. A. Bryson and P. Julian (eds.), Proceedings of the Conference on the Climate of the Eleventh and Sixteenth Centuries. National Center for Atmospheric Research, Technical Notes 63-I: 31-36. Boulder.

Wright, H. E., Jr., T. C. Winter, and H. L. Patten
1391   1963 Two Pollen Diagrams from Southeastern Minnesota; Problems in the Regional Late-Glacial and Postglacial Vegetational History. Geological Society of America Bulletin 74: 1371-1396.

Wright, H. E., Jr., and W. A. Watts, et. al.
1392   1969 Glacial and Vegetational History of Northeastern Minnesota. Minnesota Geological Survey Special Publication Series SP-II.

Yarnell, R. A.
1393   1964 Aboriginal Relationships between Culture and Plant Life in the Upper Great Lakes Region. Museum of Anthropology, University of Michigan, Anthropological Papers 23.

Yeager, D.
1394   1969 A Pollen Profile from Kennedy's Bog in Mendon Ponds Park. Rochester Academy of Science Proceedings 12: 24-45.

Zawacki, A. A., and G. Hausfater
1395   1969 Early Vegetation of the Lower Illinois Valley. Illinois State Museum Report of Investigations 17.

Ziegler, A. C.
1396   1963 Unmodified Mammal and Bird Remains from Deer Creek Cave, Elko County, Nevada. In, M. E. Shutler and R. E. Shutler, Jr., Deer Creek Cave, Elko County, Nevada. Nevada State Museum Anthropological Papers 11: 15-24.

Zumberge, J. H., and J. E. Potzger
1397   1955 Pollen Profiles, Radiocarbon Dating, and Geologic Chronology of the Lake Michigan Basin. Science 121: 309-311.

1398   1956 Late Wisconsin Chronology of the Lake Michigan Basin Correlated with Pollen Studies. Geological Society of America Bulletin 67: 271-288.

Figure I

Geographical Indexing Subdivisions

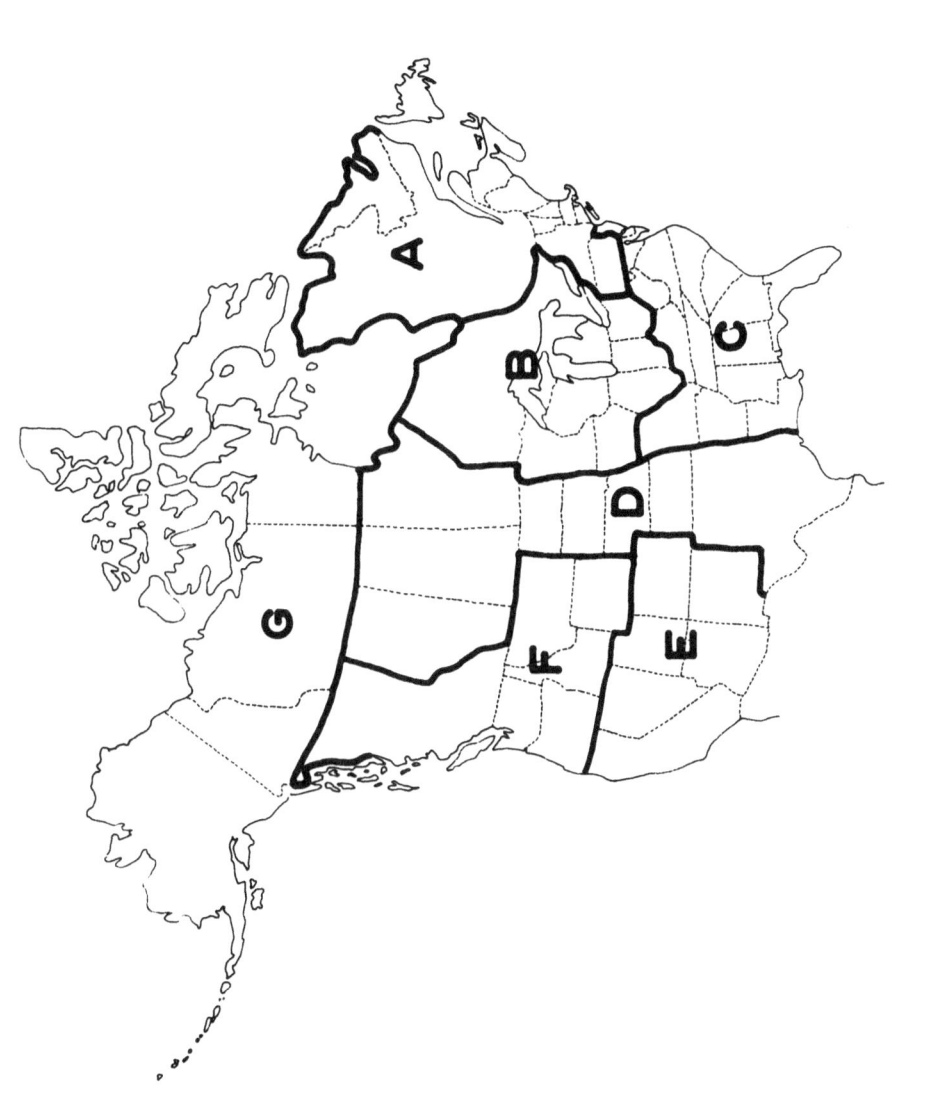

Index

The alphabetical column headings refer to the indexing subdivisions discussed in the Introduction (see also Figure 1).

A

1	154	292	424	713
2	155	293	425	718
5	163	294	432	719
21	181	295	453	722
23	184	296	461	723
32	193	297	462	725
33	195	300	474	741
44	196	301	477	748
60	203	302	478	761
63	226	303	479	762
64	227	305	480	763
69	228	307	481	765
78	229	308	483	777
79	230	310	485	778
80	245	311	486	779
93	247	315	487	798
94	268	316	488	803
96	270	328	490	804
97	272	351	503	805
104	273	352	545	806
109	274	354	552	807
110	275	356	675	827
119	276	364	676	829
129	286	379	677	832
131	287	381	685	867
133	288	383	693	872
135	289	386	699	873
136	290	420	703	896
141	291	423	704	897

B

906	1147	5	140	267
932	1150	18	141	268
935	1152	21	148	269
939	1153	23	158	274
940	1159	33	159	275
941	1181	60	160	290
942	1182	63	163	293
943	1183	64	179	296
945	1184	70	181	303
947	1198	71	184	307
968	1200	74	186	310
984	1207	77	194	311
989	1211	78	196	315
1009	1219	79	197	338
1013	1238	80	199	347
1014	1239	81	200	348
1015	1241	82	201	349
1016	1242	85	202	350
1017	1251	86	206	352
1019	1252	87	209	360
1041	1253	88	210	365
1042	1254	89	211	366
1043	1257	95	212	371
1053	1259	97	225	372
1092	1260	114	235	375
1095	1272	115	237	381
1105	1274	119	240	382
1107	1279	125	243	386
1140	1336	129	249	393
1141	1349	131	259	394
1142	1365	132	262	401
1143	1379	133	263	403
1144	1384	138	264	408
1146	1394	139	265	409

410	582	796	1003	1138
411	627	799	1004	1139
421	628	820	1005	1140
422	629	827	1006	1141
423	630	829	1008	1142
429	632	851	1010	1143
430	637	853	1011	1144
433	658	898	1012	1145
437	659	913	1018	1146
439	660	915	1020	1148
440	661	932	1022	1149
443	662	944	1026	1150
448	663	945	1027	1152
452	666	946	1028	1153
456	688	947	1032	1155
457	689	948	1033	1160
458	690	949	1034	1161
459	693	951	1036	1164
460	700	952	1043	1166
461	707	956	1048	1168
462	713	959	1055	1174
463	746	961	1070	1175
464	756	962	1079	1185
468	762	963	1080	1198
469	763	965	1081	1199
470	770	967	1083	1200
473	773	994	1084	1202
479	774	995	1085	1203
502	790	996	1089	1204
505	791	997	1095	1208
510	792	998	1133	1216
545	793	999	1135	1222
552	794	1000	1136	1223
571	795	1002	1137	1235

C

1243	1362	93	599	1347
1246	1363	131	633	1348
1248	1364	141	771	1373
1252	1367	156	872	1384
1253	1368	181	886	
1262	1369	198	923	
1263	1370	216	936	
1265	1372	224	966	
1266	1373	246	1001	
1267	1377	248	1007	
1268	1378	268	1021	
1269	1379	278	1035	
1279	1380	284	1096	
1282	1381	311	1102	
1283	1382	338	1112	
1284	1383	353	1140	
1285	1384	381	1141	
1286	1385	404	1144	
1290	1387	405	1150	
1291	1389	406	1156	
1292	1391	407	1163	
1293	1392	442	1167	
1296	1393	450	1182	
1298	1395	461	1200	
1302	1397	475	1211	
1307	1398	479	1223	
1308		483	1297	
1314		485	1299	
1339		487	1300	
1357		489	1320	
1358		498	1342	
1359		503	1344	
1360		562	1345	
1361		571	1346	

D

10	351	706	950	1200
21	368	708	969	1205
33	377	710	970	1217
49	396	711	993	1253
50	397	713	1023	1273
51	413	716	1024	1276
52	416	728	1025	1301
72	440	731	1043	1303
76	449	758	1047	1304
83	451	759	1048	1305
84	471	760	1049	1306
85	499	772	1063	1311
90	500	784	1067	1312
119	537	785	1069	1313
131	538	786	1070	1314
141	542	787	1071	1315
167	545	788	1072	1316
171	571	793	1074	1317
172	591	797	1076	1318
175	616	856	1082	1322
176	618	858	1083	1324
179	624	860	1124	1325
181	625	889	1125	1329
182	626	900	1126	1330
184	641	901	1128	1331
185	649	903	1129	1332
194	651	914	1153	1333
207	652	921	1157	1334
208	664	924	1174	1335
258	666	928	1186	1340
266	671	929	1187	1351
283	679	930	1188	1352
321	682	931	1192	1356
338	687	932	1197	1366

	E		
1376	3	99	205	374
1383	4	105	213	376
1384	7	106	214	378
	8	107	215	392
	15	108	217	395
	29	116	232	398
	30	118	244	399
	31	120	256	400
	34	122	260	402
	37	123	261	412
	38	124	277	413
	39	126	279	414
	40	130	282	426
	41	145	285	427
	42	149	298	428
	43	150	299	431
	45	151	306	438
	48	152	316	449
	51	155	321	454
	52	160	338	455
	53	161	339	461
	54	162	340	493
	55	164	341	494
	56	165	342	495
	58	166	344	497
	59	167	345	499
	61	168	355	500
	62	169	357	504
	66	170	358	521
	67	171	359	531
	75	173	361	534
	91	174	363	545
	92	185	367	546
	98	190	373	550

551	639	735	844	894
554	640	736	845	895
555	642	737	846	899
556	643	743	847	903
557	644	744	848	907
558	645	745	849	908
559	646	747	850	909
561	647	749	852	910
566	653	750	855	911
567	654	755	856	912
568	656	766	857	913
569	657	768	858	914
570	664	769	859	920
572	665	815	860	921
573	667	816	861	922
574	668	817	862	937
575	669	818	863	938
576	670	819	865	950
577	671	821	866	953
578	672	822	871	955
580	674	823	874	960
581	680	824	875	964
584	681	825	876	971
601	683	826	877	992
604	686	830	878	993
612	701	833	879	1029
613	702	834	880	1030
614	709	835	881	1037
616	710	836	882	1039
631	712	837	883	1045
634	721	838	884	1046
635	724	839	885	1054
636	733	841	888	1058
638	734	843	889	1059

			F	
1060	1126	1289	7	189
1061	1127	1309	9	190
1062	1130	1310	11	191
1063	1131	1321	12	192
1064	1134	1322	13	231
1077	1153	1323	14	251
1078	1158	1324	15	252
1082	1162	1325	16	253
1086	1165	1326	17	255
1087	1169	1327	41	256
1091	1172	1329	43	257
1093	1173	1330	46	281
1094	1176	1331	47	298
1097	1177	1332	48	303
1098	1178	1333	56	306
1099	1187	1343	59	307
1100	1189	1350	61	318
1101	1190	1355	62	321
1103	1191	1371	73	323
1104	1193	1374	99	331
1108	1194	1375	101	332
1109	1195	1384	102	333
1111	1196	1390	103	334
1113	1209	1396	113	335
1114	1210		117	336
1115	1212		119	339
1116	1213		121	340
1117	1214		142	345
1118	1215		144	369
1119	1218		146	398
1121	1228		155	399
1122	1231		160	412
1123	1264		187	413
1124	1270		188	417

418	534	653	954	1253
419	535	668	957	1256
465	536	669	992	1271
472	539	670	993	1278
482	540	673	1040	1281
484	541	705	1043	1287
496	544	714	1045	1288
506	545	729	1057	1295
507	547	732	1062	1319
508	548	751	1063	1322
509	549	759	1065	1338
511	560	767	1057	1384
512	590	783	1068	
513	592	825	1090	
514	594	854	1091	
515	595	855	1109	
516	596	856	1124	
517	597	857	1125	
518	602	858	1126	
519	604	860	1130	
520	605	861	1144	
521	607	863	1179	
522	608	864	1180	
523	609	865	1224	
524	617	870	1225	
525	619	887	1226	
526	620	888	1227	
527	625	892	1228	
528	638	902	1229	
529	642	903	1230	
530	645	914	1231	
531	646	916	1232	
532	649	925	1233	
533	650	932	1234	

G

7	241	586	730	890
19	250	587	741	893
20	254	588	752	914
21	311	589	753	917
22	317	593	754	918
23	319	594	757	919
24	320	595	772	926
25	321	596	775	927
26	322	598	776	928
27	324	600	780	929
28	325	602	781	930
111	326	603	782	931
113	346	604	789	932
119	370	605	800	934
128	386	606	801	935
134	412	610	802	958
137	434	611	806	972
157	435	621	807	973
177	436	622	809	975
181	444	623	810	976
183	445	655	811	977
184	446	678	812	978
204	447	684	813	979
218	466	691	814	980
219	467	692	856	981
220	491	694	857	982
221	492	695	858	983
222	543	696	860	985
223	545	697	861	986
233	563	698	862	987
234	564	714	863	988
236	565	717	868	989
238	579	720	869	990
239	585	729	873	991

General

992	6	307	648	1106
993	21	309	671	1110
1038	35	311	693	1120
1043	36	312	698	1132
1044	51	313	713	1142
1050	57	314	715	1143
1051	58	319	726	1151
1066	59	320	727	1152
1073	60	321	738	1154
1075	61	327	739	1155
1155	65	329	740	1156
1170	68	330	741	1201
1171	82	337	742	1220
1206	100	338	764	1221
1236	112	343	808	1223
1237	119	345	828	1240
1244	127	362	829	1245
1247	143	380	831	1249
1249	147	384	840	1252
1250	153	385	842	1253
1253	155	387	863	1275
1255	160	388	880	1279
1258	178	389	891	1280
1261	179	390	904	1328
1277	180	391	905	1353
1279	181	415	914	1384
1281	182	441	932	1386
1294	184	476	933	1388
1337	196	501	974	
1341	240	545	993	
1354	242	553	1031	
1384	271	583	1052	
	280	615	1056	
	304	647	1088	

For Product Safety Concerns and Information please contact our EU representative GPSR@taylorandfrancis.com
Taylor & Francis Verlag GmbH, Kaufingerstraße 24, 80331 München, Germany

www.ingramcontent.com/pod-product-compliance
Lightning Source LLC
Chambersburg PA
CBHW052116300426
44116CB00010B/1679